September–Dece[mber]

Day by Day with God

Rooting women's lives in the Bible

The Bible Reading Fellowship
Christina Press
Abingdon/Tunbridge Wells

The Bible Reading Fellowship
15 The Chambers, Vineyard
Abingdon OX14 3FE
brf.org.uk

The Bible Reading Fellowship (BRF) is a Registered Charity (233280)

ISBN 978 0 85746 451 4
All rights reserved

This edition © 2017 Christina Press and The Bible Reading Fellowship

Cover image © Thinkstock

Distributed in Australia by:
MediaCom Education Inc, PO Box 610, Unley, SA 5061
Tel: 1 800 811 311 | admin@mediacom.org.au

Distributed in New Zealand by:
Scripture Union Wholesale, PO Box 760, Wellington
Tel: 04 385 0421 | suwholesale@clear.net.nz

Acknowledgements
Scripture quotations taken from The Holy Bible, New International Version (Anglicised edition), copyright © 1979, 1984, 2011 by Biblica. Used by permission of Hodder & Stoughton Publishers, an Hachette UK company. All rights reserved. 'NIV' is a registered trademark of Biblica. UK trademark number 1448790.

Scripture quotations from *The Message*. Copyright © by Eugene H. Peterson 1993, 1994, 1995. Used by permission of NavPress Publishing Group.

Scripture quotations taken from the Holy Bible, New Living Translation, copyright © 1996, 2004, 2007, 2013. Used by permission of Tyndale House Publishers, Inc., Carol Stream, Illinois 60188. All rights reserved.

Scripture quotations from the Contemporary English Version. New Testament © American Bible Society 1991, 1992, 1995. Old Testament © American Bible Society 1995. Anglicisations © British & Foreign Bible Society 1996. Used by permission.

Scripture taken from the New Century Version®. Copyright © 2005 by Thomas Nelson. Used by permission. All rights reserved.

Printed by Gutenberg Press, Tarxien, Malta

Contents

Edited by **Ali Herbert** and **Jill Rattle** September–December 2017

- 6 **Have you heard of…?**
  Jill Rattle — *1–9 September*
- 16 **The 'I Ams' of Jesus**
  Chine McDonald — *10–23 September*
- 31 **Prayer**
  Catherine Butcher — *24 September–7 October*
- 46 **Confidence**
  Anne Calver — *8–21 October*
- 61 **God's ways and means**
  Jean Watson — *22–28 October*
- 69 **Galatians**
  Fiona Barnard — *29 October–11 November*
- 84 **Generations**
  Christine Leonard — *12–25 November*
- 99 **There's no place like home**
  Liz Pacey — *26 November–2 December*
- 107 **Isaiah**
  Lyndall Bywater — *3–16 December*
- 122 **Prophecies about Jesus**
  Christine Platt — *17–31 December*

Writers in this issue

Jill Rattle co-edits *Day by Day with God*. She is a retired secondary headteacher who now divides her time between Fareham and Birmingham. She loves to minister to individuals seeking spiritual support.

Chine McDonald is director of communications at the Evangelical Alliance, a trustee of the Sophia Network, Church and Media network, and author of *Am I Beautiful*, a book explaining body image and faith among Christian women'

Catherine Butcher is HOPE's Communications Director, helping churches point people to Jesus. Last year she co-authored *The Servant Queen and the King She Serves* with Mark Greene. She is an Anglican Reader in Chichester Diocese.

Anne Calver is a Baptist minister, author and speaker. Anne is passionate about word and Spirit and seeing Jesus transform lives and release people's potential. She is married to Gavin and has two children, Amelie and Daniel.

Jean Watson's work has included teaching and editing, and her writing for children and adults has been published in books and magazines and broadcast on radio and TV.

Fiona Barnard is a TEFL/ESOL teacher and staff member of Friends Intertional. She works with international students, encouraging local Christians to reach out in friendship and evangelism to make disciples.

Chris Leonard lives in Surrey with her husband. Their first two grandchildren arrived in 2015 and Chris remains busy leading creative writing courses and holidays. Her 21st book was published in November 2015.

Liz Pacey is a Reader in the Church of England and works as a freelance writer and speaker. She runs Knitwits, a charity knitting group, and is passionate about the links between knitting and spirituality.

Lyndall Bywater is a freelance writer, trainer and consultant in all things related to prayer. She lives in Canterbury with her husband.

Christine Platt loves living in New Zealand. As well as local church ministry, she travels to Timor-Leste regularly to teach English and the Bible.

Ali Herbert and Jill Rattle write...

Some years pass by fairly quietly when not much happens, but 2017 is proving a momentous year for us and our family. Ali has become a student again (the proud owner of a 16–25 Student railcard!) attending lectures and writing essays as she begins training for ordination. Jill, after living in the same house for 39 years, has begun the process of relocating from Fareham to Birmingham. For both of us it's something of a journey into the unknown. It's not, of course, as much of a journey into the unknown as that of the patriarch Abraham or the disciples responding to Jesus' call, but nevertheless it's a slightly daunting challenge to step out of our comfort zone and follow that inner voice that calls us onto unfamiliar ground. To say we've both experienced some nervousness is not an exaggeration. Have we heard God's voice aright? Are we up to it? Will we cope with the changes? How will it affect family and friends?

For that reason, we are so glad that our new contributor, Anne Calver, has taken on the topic of 'Confidence'. She takes us through different contexts including confidence in stepping out, confidence in calling and confidence in obedience. In doing so she paints a wonderful picture of the confidence we can have in God in any circumstances, whether peaceful, uncertain or stormy.

'Trust in the Lord with all your heart and lean not on your own understanding; in all your ways submit to him and he will make your paths straight' (Proverbs 3:5–6, NIV).

Following on from Anne, Jean Watson looks at the ways and means our kind God uses to build the confidence of faith in us. And the rest of our contributors, taking us through Old and New Testaments, show us why we can step out in our Christian lives with boldness and confidence, sharing and reflecting the good news that God loves us, Jesus died for us and the Holy Spirit lives within us.

Have you heard of…?

Jill Rattle writes:

We know that Western society is held in thrall to celebrity culture. What seems to matter is how many people know who you are, for whatever reason, good or bad, and social media has made it possible for the most unlikely people to be known by thousands, if not millions of others. Some children often hope just to be 'famous' when they grow up.

Characters in the Bible were also not immune to 'celebrity envy': King Saul was driven to murderous rage by the popular chant: 'Saul has slain his thousands and David his tens of thousands' (1 Samuel 18:7); Jesus' disciples earned his rebuke for squabbling over their relative importance (Luke 9:46), and the ambitious mother of James and John wanted the highest positions for them (Matthew 20:20–28).

The Bible is full of important, larger-than-life characters whose stories echo powerfully down the centuries and whose names we all know: Adam, Abraham, Moses, Jonah, Matthew, Peter, Paul and so on. But throughout the pages of Scripture there are many lesser-known men and women whose stories are briefly touched on but who played an important part in God's wonderful work and in some cases changed history: the midwives who prevented genocide, the Hebrew sisters who changed the law, the Roman official whose hospitality resulted in hundreds being healed and following Jesus.

So, I thought, let's spend a couple of weeks reading about the daughters of Zelophehad; Shiphrah and Puah; the Food Bank Managers; Shobi, Machir and Barzillai; Publius; Hur; Josiah; the Sons of Korah, and Deborah.

I'm not sure that Deborah deserves to be listed under the 'lesser-known' category as she is such a magnificent figure in the Bible, though I can't remember any sermons about her.

Even in church we can be 'seduced' by celebrity culture. There are church leaders who are widely known, admired and followed. That's not necessarily wrong if, like Deborah, their whole purpose is to give the glory back to God, but as someone said, 'The bigger the leader, the bigger the target on their back.' We need to pray hard for those in the limelight.

And all of us, Jesus' followers who are not in the limelight, can learn from these lesser-known Bible figures that each of us is essential to the outworking of God's loving purposes.

FRIDAY 1 SEPTEMBER NUMBERS 27:1–11

Noah and her sisters

So Moses brought their case before the Lord, and the Lord said to him, 'What Zelophehad's daughters are saying is right. You must certainly give them property as an inheritance among their father's relatives and give their father's inheritance to them.' (NIV)

Noah—not the man in the ark, but one of the five daughters of Zelophehad: Mahlah, Noah, Hoglah, Milkah and Tirzah. They were very special women; with the exception of Serah, daughter of Asher, they are the only women listed among the descendants of the tribes and clans of Israel (Numbers 26:33). And what a feisty, assertive, bold group of women they were.

Their father, Zelophehad, had died without a son and heir during the long wandering of the Israelites in the desert. Disaster! When Moses came to parcel out land for the tribes' inheritance, there'd be nothing for the Z family. Girls didn't count. Just accept it. But not these girls. I imagine it went something like this... 'Accept it? No way!' snaps Mahlah. 'We are not going to let them walk all over us.'

'Right,' agrees Noah, 'it's just not fair. Why should our family be penalised, our clan name disappear because we're not men!' Together they make the audacious decision to present their case to the great leader of their nation, Moses. And all credit to them, they do it! Together, no doubt standing very close, they approach the judgement seat of Moses, in front of the priests, the leaders and the whole assembly. Five women amid thousands of men.

They present their case calmly, logically, persuasively. They know they are asking for something that would seriously upset the prevailing customs and culture. What odds would a bookmaker have given them on succeeding? But they do! Moses listens to them with respect and then, wise man of God that he is, he takes the situation to God in prayer. And the Lord confirms his decision. The daughters of Zelophehad win their case and the law of inheritance is altered in Israel. The girls have it!

In 2017 groups of Christian women, working together in the strength of the Spirit, can still bring about change and social justice.

JILL RATTLE

SATURDAY 2 SEPTEMBER — **EXODUS 1:8–20**

Shiphrah and Puah

'When you are helping the Hebrew women during childbirth on the delivery stool, if you see that the baby is a boy, kill him; but if it is a girl, let her live.' The midwives, however, feared God and did not do what the king of Egypt had told them to do; they let the boys live. (NIV)

In an article in *The Nursing Times*, Helen Lockett wrote: 'For nurses with true leadership qualities, this will include having the courage to challenge people when they see wrongdoing. It is about showing that there is another way to do things, thinking in extraordinary ways and finding solutions to challenges.'

Many nurses in the past and present have lived up to that ideal. One was British nurse Edith Cavell who, in World War I, saved the lives of soldiers on *both* sides and was executed by the Germans as a spy. In 2011 Lance Corporal Kylie Watson was awarded the Military Cross after risking her life under heavy fire to treat two wounded Afghan soldiers.

Two biblical nurse heroines were the midwives, Shiphrah and Puah. Pharaoh had become terrified by the growing numbers of Hebrews, fearing a threat to his dynasty. Ordered by Pharaoh to kill the Hebrew baby boys at birth 'on the delivery stool', they refused. They were women who feared God and put the highest priority on the value of life. But what extraordinary courage they showed! To defy the direct commands of the Pharaoh—unthinkable! But they did it. Amazing!

When Pharaoh discovered they were disobeying him. he summoned them before him. I can't imagine a more terrifying experience for those women but, quick-wittedly, they made the excuse that Hebrew women gave birth so quickly that they couldn't get there in time for the delivery! And he accepted it! Together Shiphrah and Puah helped prevent genocide. How appropriate that their names mean 'brightness' and 'splendour'.

That same courage and dedication to what is right should be our hallmark too. But, as with the Hebrew midwives, those qualities will be in direct proportion to our faith and trust in God.

Lord, fill us with your courage, that our lives may show something of the brightness and splendour of Jesus.

JILL RATTLE

SUNDAY 3 SEPTEMBER — ACTS 6:1–7

The Food Bank Managers

'Brothers and sisters, choose seven men from among you who are known to be full of the Spirit and wisdom.' (NIV)

Philip, Procorus, Nicanor, Timon, Parmenas and Nicolas: these six men were chosen to assist Stephen in the early church food bank. A dispute had arisen because the Christian Greek widows weren't getting the same food allowance as the Christian Jewish widows. The twelve apostles drew all the disciples together and quite reasonably pointed out that their priority was preaching and teaching and they didn't have time 'to wait on tables' as well. So they delegated.

All leaders need to delegate, for if they take on everything, it will inevitably lead to burn-out.

I recall in a newly planted church seeing a leader, shortly after preaching, mopping the toilet floors. In one way I applaud this because she was modelling Jesus who cleaned the filthy feet of his disciples; but as that church grew, the members would surely need to appoint others to do the practical jobs while the leaders did the preaching and teaching.

However, what shouts out to me from this Bible passage is that the criteria for selection of the food bank managers was that they should be 'full of the Holy Spirit and wisdom'. This tells me that whatever tasks you and I take on in the church, we need the filling of the Holy Spirit, giving us the wisdom to do it so well that we bring glory to God. It also tells me how highly God values *all* service done in Jesus' name. Perhaps we are in danger sometimes of seeing some church roles as 'spiritual' (preaching) and some 'practical' (making the coffee). Not so. Everything we do in and for the body of Christ is spiritual. For instance, the hospitality a newcomer receives when she/he comes through the doors can make all the difference to how receptive they are to the teaching they hear.

Whatever jobs you do in the church, ask the Holy Spirit to fill you and give you wisdom—to do them so well that others will catch a sight of Jesus.

JILL RATTLE

MONDAY 4 SEPTEMBER — 2 SAMUEL 17:27–29

Shobi, Machir and Barzillai

> [They] brought beds and blankets, bowls and jugs filled with wheat, barley, flour, roasted grain, beans and lentils, honey, and curds and cheese from the flocks and herds. They presented all this to David and his army to eat, 'because,' they said, 'the army must be starved and exhausted and thirsty out in this wilderness.' (*The Message*)

David was experiencing one of the most painful experiences of his life. His beloved son Absalom had turned traitor and was trying to usurp the throne: David and his entourage had been forced to flee from him. They'd been marching through appalling conditions in the desert. Now emotionally and physically exhausted, with no resources left, David stopped at the little town of Mahanaim. By coincidence this was the place where, many years before, Jacob had had his vision of angels.

David was certainly in need of angels! And he got them—in the form of Shobi, Machir and Barzillai. Their hospitality was amazingly generous. They seem to have set up a luxury camp (glamping?) for David and his men. Not only did they bring all the food they could possibly eat and all the equipment to cook it with, but beds and washing facilities! David must have been so grateful to be able to relax a little and regain his strength. These three men served God by providing support to David, God's servant.

Generous giving should be the hallmark of every local church and every Christian. We are called to be constantly on the lookout for those to whom we can offer help and support. That support is especially needed for those in full-time Christian ministry at home or abroad, who cannot do their work without the resources provided by other Christians. One leader I know was feeling very discouraged because funds were lacking to complete a project. Then the phone rang: the money was offered. In such ways we can share in each other's ministries.

God does not expect us to meet *all* needs everywhere. He *does* expect us to ask him daily which needs he wants us personally to supply.

Holy Spirit, thank you for the privilege of serving others. Please prompt me to see clearly today those people and situations that you want me to help.

JILL RATTLE

TUESDAY 5 SEPTEMBER   **ACTS 28:1–10**

Publius

He welcomed us to his home and showed us generous hospitality for three days. (NIV)

My parents had the most wonderful gift of hospitality. Although my mum was not a great cook, the dinner table was always crowded with laughing guests (not at the food!); my dad maintained the small swimming pool at the bottom of the garden almost entirely for the benefit of visitors. They both shone the light of Jesus.

Many years after they died and many miles from their home, I met the minister of a very welcoming church. In conversation I learnt, to both our astonishment, that as a teenager with his youth club friends he had often swum in my parents' pool and that their inclusive love and hospitality had been a major factor in his choosing to be a Christian. Many others have since met Jesus as a result of his ministry.

In yesterday's passage David and his men received generous hospitality; in today's, centuries later, Paul and his shipwrecked fellows benefit from the wonderful welcome and hospitality of Publius, the chief official on Malta. There is no indication of any ulterior motive in Publius' invitation but we're told that Publius' father was sick and when Paul heard this he visited him and healed him in Jesus' name. As a result many others on the island also encountered the healing power of Jesus.

Publius had no idea when he invited Paul to stay that his generous hospitality would be the key that unlocked God's grace throughout the community. Tradition has it that Publius became the first Bishop of Malta. Whether he did or not, opening his doors that day transformed his and his family's life and that of many others too.

I wonder if you can look back on people who opened their doors and their hearts to you, and encouraged you on your Christian journey.

Thank you, Lord, for those who have offered us Christian hospitality. Please give us the same gift and, in your grace, multiply the blessing down the years.
                                                                                                   JILL RATTLE

WEDNESDAY 6 SEPTEMBER **EXODUS 17:8–16**

Hur

As long as Moses held up his hands, the Israelites were winning, but whenever he lowered his hands, the Amalekites were winning. (NIV)

One thing I love about the church I attend is the prayer support before the Sunday services for those who are on the 'frontline': those who are preaching, leading worship or young people's work, or offering welcome at the door; they are all prayed for in turn. They are 'held up' to God for his blessing and protection.

Our passage today describes the critical time when the Israelites, on their journey towards the promised land, meet for the first time an enemy army, the fearsome Amalekites. Their great leader, Moses, stands on a hill above the battle mêlée, while his younger lieutenant, Joshua, leads the fight below. Moses' task in the sight of the people is to stand with hands raised to God, interceding on their behalf. His brother, Aaron, stands with him and so does a man named Hur. While Moses conducts his powerful ministry, hands held high, the Israelites prevail. But as the hours pass, Moses wearies, hands dropping in exhaustion—and the Amalekites gain the advantage. Aaron lifts up his brother's right hand and Hur steps forward and lifts the left. Together they support Moses and as they do the Israelites win the battle, the Amalekites are put to flight.

We know very little more about Hur (he appears again briefly in Exodus 24); he does not have the same profile or status as Moses, Aaron and Joshua, but without his physical and moral support that day, Moses' work would not have been accomplished and victory would not have been won. Hur was there for his leader.

Someone said, borrowing an image from car racing, that every Christian leader needs a 'pit-stop team', a group of people who are 'there' for them at every turn and twist of the journey. Are you willing to be a Hur?

Without your support, someone's ministry could be in trouble.

JILL RATTLE

THURSDAY 7 SEPTEMBER   **2 KINGS 22:1–3, 8–13**

Josiah

[Josiah] lived the way God wanted. He kept straight on the path blazed by his ancestor David, not one step to either left or right. (*The Message*)

My daughter and her husband were exercised as to what to name their second child, a boy. Nothing quite fitted. Then in the middle of one night she woke with a name: 'Josiah'. She knew he was one of the Old Testament kings but was he a good or bad one? After all, many of them 'did evil in the sight of the Lord'. She had to get out of bed and look Josiah up! The words quoted above reassured her it was a good choice: 'he lived the way God wanted'.

Josiah succeeded as King of Judah at the age of eight, after his father's assassination. Both father and grandfather had set him a terrible example but somehow by the grace of God (and perhaps through the nurture of his mother?) Josiah grew up a fine, godly man. At 24 he set about bringing his people back to the worship of and obedience to the one true God.

The catalyst for Josiah's mission was the rediscovery of 'the Book of the Law' and the powerful effect reading it had on him: he was horrified at what the Law revealed about sin, the sins of his people and ancestors, and judgement to come. Immediately he called for an urgent prayer meeting. 'Ask God what we must do in response,' he urged. And once he knew what God wanted him to do, he obeyed without delay.

God's response to Josiah taking his Law seriously, and his humble repentance, was to promise him peace in his lifetime. And so it was. Josiah not only started well, he finished well.

What a good example Josiah is to us as Jesus' followers. When we open the word of God, do we let it penetrate our hearts and show up anything we need to confess and repent of, for which we can then receive his forgiveness?

Lord, when we hear your voice through your word, the Bible, help us to respond and obey so that we may receive your peace. Help us to 'finish well'.
JILL RATTLE

The Sons of Korah

Better is one day in your courts than a thousand elsewhere; I would rather be a doorkeeper in the house of my God than dwell in the tents of the wicked. (NIV)

One of the last to leave church that Sunday, I chatted with the caretaker standing with his keys ready to lock up. In the course of conversation I discovered he wasn't the paid caretaker but a volunteer on the rota: his normal job was the boss of one of the largest businesses in the UK. My reaction? Goodness, his real job is so much more important than just caretaking! God's reaction? I think his would be rather different: 'If both those jobs are done in my name and for my kingdom, I value them equally.' God's perspective is not ours. Sadly our values are often not his.

In 1 Chronicles 24—26, David divides up the descendants of Aaron into different groups for ministry in the temple. The Sons of Korah are among the door- or gatekeepers. They were the ancient equivalent of security guards, ensuring the safety of God's house, keeping order and keeping out anything or anybody that might defile the place.

Tragically some churches today need to employ security guards, but thankfully they are not tasked to ensure the spiritual fitness of those entering. How many of us would get in most Sundays? Having said that, how important it is that we come into church empty-handed and open-hearted, recognising our spiritual poverty and eager to be filled with God's forgiveness and grace.

How important it is also to realise, as we take our seats, that not one of us is more important than any other in the sight of God. He rates us all as important!

Beautiful Psalm 84 must have been written by a son of Korah: it brims over with passion and delight for this place where constant praise is raised to the wonderful God who favours, shields, rescues, strengthens and transforms.

To what extent does your church reflect Psalm 84? Is there a 'doorkeeper' you can affirm and encourage?

JILL RATTLE

SATURDAY 9 SEPTEMBER   **JUDGES 4:4–5; 5:1–9**

Deborah

'Villagers in Israel would not fight; they held back until I, Deborah, arose… a mother in Israel. God chose new leaders when war came to the city gates… My heart is with Israel's princes, with the willing volunteers among the people. Praise the Lord!' (NIV)

One of the things that delights me as I move into 'older age' is to see younger Christian women of great ability and faith come into leadership roles inside and outside the church. In the last few weeks I have listened to three women preaching with power and authority, God's anointing clearly upon them. When I was a teenager that would have been a rare opportunity.

Of course, God has been anointing women to do great things for him for generations. And one of those was the amazing Deborah. We know nothing about her early life but her parents named her Deborah, 'the bee', which in those times was considered to be the most intelligent of creatures. She must have been, because she rose to become a judge, a ruler over Israel. God gave her outstanding mental and spiritual gifts: wisdom and discernment, leadership and faith. She sat under her palm tree and dispensed wise justice. She was a powerful prophet too—all other prophets of the time deferred to her. A prophet is defined as one who discerns the purposes of God and declares them to others. When Deborah spoke, everyone listened and obeyed!

God raised Deborah up at a time when the people of Israel, after 20 years of oppression at the hands of the King of Canaan, were broken, defeated and listless—their army was pretty useless too. Under God, Deborah turned all that around and led her people to such a decisive victory over Canaan that they had peace for the next 40 years.

We may not all be Deborahs but let's pray for more and more leaders in the mould of Deborah to be anointed in our time, women of faith and ability who can do mighty things for God.

Pray for a woman you know in a leadership role, that she may be filled with and led by the Holy Spirit. And pray for more!

JILL RATTLE

The 'I Ams' of Jesus

Chine McDonald writes…

'I am—yet what I am none cares or knows'. These are the opening words of the famous poem, 'I Am', by John Clare. These words have been swirling around in my head as I have written this set of notes on the 'I Am' sayings of Jesus. The identity of Christ is far from something that no one cares about or knows. In fact, the very nature of the Messiah was debated long before the incarnation and continues to be debated today in churches and academic and theological settings. These sayings of Jesus touch on his identity, the nature of God, the Trinity, of life, death and resurrection. They are amazing reminders about what our own identities are as followers of Christ and how who he is has a very real impact on our daily lives, how we see ourselves and how we relate to the world around us—a world that so often makes us feel unsure about who we are.

In our reading over the next fortnight, we will explore the seven famous 'I Am' sayings of Jesus: 'I am the bread of life', 'I am the light of the world', 'I am the good shepherd', 'I am the door', 'I am the true vine', 'I am the way and the truth and the life', and 'I am the resurrection and the life'. Along the way, we will also look at some statements about the identity of Jesus, including Jesus as the Word made flesh.

The John Clare poem above is one of those often recited at funerals, words spoken at the end of life. But in writing these notes, I have been struck again by just how amazing the hope we have in Jesus is, what a difference the person he is makes to our lives right now. He is the resurrection and the life—by putting our faith in him we too will not die but have eternal life. But we don't have to wait to step into that to which he has called us, because Jesus is also the one through whom we can have life in all its fullness. And that abundant life starts now.

SUNDAY 10 SEPTEMBER   **JOHN 1:1–14**

My favourite word

In the beginning was the Word, and the Word was with God, and the Word was God. He was with God in the beginning. Through him all things were made; without him nothing was made that has been made. In him was life, and that life was the light of all mankind. The light shines in the darkness, and the darkness has not overcome it. (NIV)

I love words. My favourite is 'brouhaha'; closely followed by 'nonchalant' and 'susurration'. As a writer, I love the shape of words, I love the sounds of them as they roll off the tongue. I love ordering and reordering them until I get the meaning I'm intending to convey. I love how words can paint a thousand pictures; how they can bring comfort to those in their dying hours, express the deepest feelings through those three simple words 'I love you'. Words have the power to build up and the ability to break down. Today's passage takes on an even more beautiful meaning for me as a lover of words. The idea that God's Word was there in the beginning, that the Word was with him and was him.

Words have the power to inhabit the feelings we have and the things that we want to express. And here we see the Word inhabit the flesh—God made incarnate and dwelling among us. What does the word 'incarnation' mean for us in our daily lives? What difference does it make to our daily commute, our to-do lists, piles of ironing?

The incarnation means he, the Word, is right there with us in the midst of all of it. Incarnation means inhabiting the whole of human life, taking on the sufferings and the pains but also the daily facts of being human—hunger, boredom, frustration, joy, illness—from the sublime to the mundane.

God chooses not to be with us solely in the good times, but in those times when we are at our lowest; lost in the depths of horror with seemingly no way out. What a glorious Saviour we have in Jesus, the servant king, the Word made flesh.

God incarnate, we are astonished that you would die for us and now live in us through all that life throws at us. Thank you for loving us so much that you would become like us. Amen

CHINE MCDONALD

MONDAY 11 SEPTEMBER   **JOHN 9:1–7**

The night is dark

'While I am in the world, I am the light of the world.' (NIV)

After much resistance, I became a follower of the hit TV show Game of Thrones. It is truly bleak, harrowing and violent; watching it is like peering into the dark brutality of humankind. I wouldn't recommend it if you are easily squeamish. One of the repeated phrases throughout the series uttered by followers of the religion of the 'lord of light' is: 'The night is dark and full of terrors.'

This haunting phrase has occasionally felt as if it was referring to real life rather than fiction. The world seems so dark at times. There is darkness in personal tragedies and pains we experience. We watch those we love go through dark, difficult times, we hear of wars and rumours of wars; senseless killings, freak accidents and terrorist atrocities on unimaginable scales.

All over the western world today, people will be remembering 9/11—which remains a turning point in world history. Many countries around the world have become used to terrorism as part of their daily lives and indeed humankind throughout history has faced such waves of mass killings. But it seemed that 9/11 was a reminder that such things can happen to people like us.

In all these things, we may question where God is. Where is his light in all this darkness? Jesus' comforting words come straight after his encounter with a man born blind. His blindness is not because of his sin or any sins his parents had committed. 'But this happened so that the works of God might be displayed in him,' Jesus says. As dark and full of terror the world often feels, it is often at these times that I am blown away by seeing God's light break through.

Dear Lord, help me never to despair even though all around me looks dark. Help me to look to you, for you are the Lord of all light, the God of hope.

CHINE MCDONALD

TUESDAY 12 SEPTEMBER — HEBREWS 13:5–8

Never-changing God

Jesus Christ is the same yesterday and today and for ever. (NIV)

Have you ever read aloud all the promises that God has spoken to us? The Bible is full of God's vows to his people—from the ancient accounts of his presence among Israel to the promises given by the Word made flesh in Jesus to the beautiful passages in Revelation that talk of God making all things new, wiping every tear from our eyes. Declaring those words with boldness reminds us of the amazing hope that we have in our God.

For those who grew up in safe, loving homes, the promises our parents made to us—of an ice cream or a new toy or whatever it was—meant something, because there was an implicit trust that we had in our parents. How often we forget God's promises to us; and even when we remember, how often do we forget that God is 'good for his word'?

Throughout the Bible accounts, God introduces himself as the God of Abraham, Isaac and Jacob. In effect, he is listing his referees, reminding us of what he has done before and listing those who can vouch for his goodness in their lives. The promises may have come later than anticipated and not in the manner in which they were expected, but they did come to pass.

Today's verse is an amazing reminder that God never changes. Not only does the whole Bible stand as a reference to his goodness and consistency but it shows us that he is the one constant through life's ecstatic highs and earth-shattering lows. What an amazing comfort it is for us to know that God is faithful; that he will never leave us or forsake us, that he is the same yesterday, today and for ever.

Lord, thank you for your steadfast love for us that remains steady even amid the stormy seas of life. Please help us to fix our eyes on you and not be swayed by all that is going on around us.

CHINE MCDONALD

WEDNESDAY 13 SEPTEMBER   **JOHN 14:1–6**

Our divine sat-nav

Jesus answered, 'I am the way and the truth and the life. No one comes to the Father except through me.' (NIV)

I've never been very good at directions. I am very thankful for the direction function on my phone. You might think I would never get lost? But even while watching and listening intently to the phone's directions, I take a wrong turning and have to find the right path again. I recently had a hair-raising driving experience in the south of France en route to a family wedding. I was already nervous driving on the wrong side of the road in an unfamiliar hire car; and then the sat-nav had one of those frustrating episodes where it just was not taking us to our destination. It re-routed and re-routed with me and my passengers becoming increasingly agitated as the time for the wedding arrived and passed.

So much of our Christian lives involve re-routing. In God's grace and the free will he has given us, we are free to take the wrong turnings if that is what we insist on. But today's passage is a reminder that Jesus is the 'way', the route we are supposed to follow. Perhaps we might look to other routes as a means of getting to where we ultimately want to go. Some follow the route of ambition and career, others the path of serving those who are most in need. Some follow the road of family life and others the hedonistic way. But all of these—no matter how good they are in and of themselves—lead to a dead end. 'I am the way,' Jesus says.

It's such a lovely feeling when you find the right path to where you are going, having taken the wrong turning and been re-routed. You go from a sense of frustration and all being lost to the conviction that everything is as it should be.

Jesus, we thank you that you are the only way, the right way. Help us to never take the wrong turning and follow your path. Show us what that means in our daily lives.

CHINE MCDONALD

THURSDAY 14 SEPTEMBER   **JOHN 14:6–14**

Truth and justice

Jesus answered, 'I am the way and the truth and the life. No one comes to the Father except through me.' (NIV)

In recent years, there has been an explosion of TV and radio/podcast broadcasts which look at the truth behind shocking crimes and miscarriages of justice. Making a Murderer and the podcast Serial have gained huge followings as it seems people just cannot get enough of finding out the truth. Both explore the crimes that led to the imprisonment of men accused of committing them, but hint at possible miscarriages of justice. It seems we are becoming increasingly fascinated and obsessed with justice.

In today's passage, truth and justice are combined in Jesus' 'I am' statement. He alone is the truth, he says. But he also says that no one comes to the Father except through him. We know that God is perfect and abhors sin. And we also know that we are broken, sinful people. We know therefore that we cannot find a way to God on our own. We also know that God is just and that the wages of sin is death (see Romans 3:23). Because we are sinful people, the only just response is for our sins to be dealt with in some way, for us to be held accountable for the things we have done.

But it is an absolute 'scandal of grace' that God himself, through Jesus, chooses to take on our brokenness, sin and shame. Because of what he has done for us—his incarnation, death and resurrection—we have not been treated as our sins deserve. There is no way we could come to the Father except through Jesus. What an amazing gift our salvation is!

Lord, help us to keep our eyes fixed on you, through whom we have salvation.
CHINE MCDONALD

FRIDAY 15 SEPTEMBER JOHN 11:1–25

A matter of life and death

'Lord,' Martha said to Jesus, 'if you had been here, my brother would not have died. But I know that even now God will give you whatever you ask.' Jesus said to her, 'Your brother will rise again.' (NIV)

As I write, I am on the way to the hospital where a close family member is in her final days after a long battle with cervical cancer. These visits over the past few months as she has been in hospital have been unbearably difficult at times. In recent days, we have been informed that there is nothing more to be done. As she has come to terms with this, so have we. We have as a family started to prepare for her departure. In those short visits to her hospital room in recent months, I have felt a real sense of God's presence, and a clear peace that I did not know was possible.

In today's passage, we read about Lazarus' sisters in the aftermath of his death. When Jesus finally arrives, Martha says, 'Lord, if you had been there, my brother would not have died.' You can feel the pain in her voice, the anguish. Where *were* you?

But the first thing Jesus tells Martha is that her brother will rise again. She thinks he is just giving her a platitude like everyone else, one of those things you say when someone has just died. But she doesn't understand Jesus' words. Yes, Lazarus will rise again that very day. And then after death, he will live eternally because of Jesus' sacrifice on the cross. 'I am the resurrection and the life,' Jesus tells her. Death can seem so final when we watch the earthly bodies of our loved ones fade away. But thank God that this is not the end. Thank God that death is swallowed up in victory.

Thank God for his victory over death and the opportunity to live life in all its fullness today, but also the gift of life even after we die.

CHINE MCDONALD

This changes everything

'I am the resurrection and the life.' (NIV)

Have you heard it said that there is more evidence for Jesus' resurrection from both Christian and non-Christian sources than any other event in history?

Do you, like me, get frustrated by the refusal of non-Christian friends to admit that the life, death and resurrection of Jesus is historical fact? So many do not believe, likening the existence of Jesus to belief in Father Christmas, fairies and the Loch Ness monster. A recent study called *Talking Jesus*, commissioned by the Evangelical Alliance, the Church of England and HOPE, found that 40% of people are not even convinced that Jesus was a real person. If so many do not even believe Jesus walked the earth, how can they believe he was raised from the dead and that this fact makes a difference to their lives? How vital it is, then, that we his followers show the difference the risen Lord has made to us.

As many theologians have commented, the resurrection is the fact upon which the Christian faith hinges. It is of 'first importance', as Paul writes in 1 Corinthians 15:3. This is more than just about the historicity of Jesus' death and resurrection. Our return to John 11 today shows Jesus declaring that in him is the resurrection and the life. The earthly death and resurrection of his human body means that those of us who place our faith in him can also have that resurrection and that life. If Christ did not die, then we are living our lives burdened by our sins. Because of his life, death and resurrection, we are free—unchained, unburdened by what has gone before, called out of brokenness and invited into the fullness of life.

What does Jesus' proclamation that he is the resurrection and the life change in my daily life? Everything.

Read 1 Corinthians 15 for more on the importance of the resurrection.

CHINE MCDONALD

SUNDAY 17 SEPTEMBER JOHN 10:1–10

Abundant life

'I am the door, and the person who enters through me will be saved and will be able to come in and go out and find pasture. A thief comes to steal and kill and destroy, but I came to give life—life in all its fullness.' (NCV)

This is one of my favourite verses in the Bible. I love the promise that Jesus has come to give us life in all its fullness—abundant life. So often Christians are characterised for what we are 'against'. So often the world sees us as anti-fun, as judgemental, hypocritical, dour party-poopers. But this is so far from what we are supposed to be. We are supposed to be the good news people, the life and soul of the party—the ones living life in all its fullness.

But what does life in all its fullness look like to the outside world? And what does it mean for us in our daily lives?

In this passage Jesus, who has come to give us abundant life, describes the alternative to himself. He describes the 'thief' who comes to 'steal and kill and destroy'.

What are the things in your life that are stealing your joy, killing your hope and destroying your future? Life in all its fullness is a life that does not look as if it has been robbed. It is a life that looks whole. It is a life that recognises on a daily basis that we are people of hope, saved from our brokenness and invited to walk in new life. It looks like thinking of ourselves as fearfully and wonderfully made, children of God who have a hope and a future in him. Let us enter in through Jesus to be saved and find pasture. Because life in all its fullness looks amazing.

Consider making a list of the things in your life that do not demonstrate life in all its fullness. Pray that God might help you walk in the full light of his love.

CHINE MCDONALD

MONDAY 18 SEPTEMBER   **JOHN 15:1–4**

Active remaining

'Remain in me, as I also remain in you. No branch can bear fruit by itself; it must remain in the vine. Neither can you bear fruit unless you remain in me.' (NIV)

The European Union referendum of June 2016 was a defining moment for our nation. Regardless of which side you were on, the campaign drew clear lines between communities. As someone who is interested in communications and advertising, the word 'leave' seems active to me. It felt that it would mean *doing* something. The word 'remain', on the other hand, in terms of campaigning and communication, seems far more passive. To remain means to stay the same, and as far as the EU was concerned, it meant maintaining the status quo. In today's passage the word 'remain' does not seem passive. The remaining here is about actively sticking to Jesus—the true vine.

My husband and I recently joined the National Trust and have enjoyed exploring some of the beautiful stately homes and gardens across the UK. Wandering through these gardens, we often find sprawling vines that clamber their way around and up the garden walls. I rarely stop and think about how each vine branch is connecting to the life coursing through the vine. It's an amazing image of the unity that exists between the branches and the vine, and between us and the Christ, the true vine.

The branches cling to the vine in a way that is active. For them it is a matter of life and death. Should they become separated from the vine, they will wither and die. Disconnecting or choosing to 'leave' is not an option. They have no choice but to remain.

What would our lives as Christ followers look like if we remembered how actively we need to remain in the vine? This is not about passivity or just hanging around, loosely connecting nominally to God. To abide in him is everything. It is all we need to do to live whole and fruitful lives.

Lord, help us to stick fast to you, the true vine.

CHINE MCDONALD

TUESDAY 19 SEPTEMBER   **REVELATION 1:1–8**

Beginning and end

'I am the Alpha and the Omega,' says the Lord God, 'who is, and who was, and who is to come, the Almighty.' (NIV)

The week before the rest of my undergraduate friends started university, I and a group of others who were coming up to study theology had to attend an intensive week of learning New Testament Greek. This was a language that was totally alien to us, but would form a foundational part of biblical studies. For those of us who have grown up in Christian churches, we get used to God being described as 'the Alpha and Omega'. But what does it mean, and what difference does it make to our lives if he is?

I am reminded of that song in one of my favourite films, *The Sound of Music*. Maria is teaching the children to sing and tells them: 'When you read you begin with ABC. When you sing, you begin with Do-Re-Mi.' When you start to learn Greek, you start at the very beginning—alpha, the first word of the Greek alphabet. When time begins, it starts with the Creator God who is himself beyond time and outside time. Just like your first foray into the Greek alphabet ends at the word 'omega', so the end of time will be wrapped up by God when his kingdom comes on earth.

We are living in the now-and-not-yet, the in-between times while we live in the light of the resurrection; but we won't see the fulfilment of his kingdom on earth until he comes again. God as both Alpha and Omega means that there is nothing in which we can find more security, wholeness, life. God is the beginning of all things and the end of all our searching. While we may spend much of our lives trying to find meaning or truth or value or identity, we realise that as Alpha and Omega, our creator God is enough.

Lord God Almighty, help our unbelief—those times when we do not trust wholly and completely in you. Help us to remember that you are the end of all our searching.

CHINE MCDONALD

WEDNESDAY 20 SEPTEMBER **JOHN 8:48–58**

Who do you think you are?

'Very truly I tell you,' Jesus answered, 'before Abraham was born, I am!' (NIV)

Jesus was never confused about who he was. In the encounter with the religious leaders described in this passage, Jesus is accused of being a demon-possessed Samaritan. I love the ease with which he says, 'I am not' but goes on to make clear what he *is*. And his claims are bold. Whoever obeys what he says will never see death, he tells them. Imagine the audacity of it! 'Who do you think you are?' they exclaim.

How often do we as Christ followers have the boldness to declare our true identity as sons and daughters of the living God? Who do we think we are? Society tends to ask us to name our identities, identities which often compete with each other. Speaking personally as a first-generation immigrant, I struggle with the question of whether I am Nigerian or British. I am a Londoner, I'm a woman and a feminist, a millennial, a keen baker and home chef. I am a friend, daughter, sister and a wife. I'm a boss and an employee. My newspaper of choice is the *Guardian*.

So often the world—particularly through the influence of social media—asks us to choose our tribe. Who are we exactly? Where does our identity lie? Our identity should be firmly rooted in Jesus.

Thank God that Jesus, the one in whom we find our never-changing identity, is sure of who he is and absolutely certain of who we are. Thank God that he sees us not as we see ourselves.

In our verse Jesus claims that he existed long before the present moment: but he, the Ancient of Days, lives not only in the past but is with us today, right now, right here. 'I am!' he says. And because he is, we are, too.

Lord, thank you for your death and resurrection for us. Thank you that you go on living in us and through us today. May we recognise our true identity as your children rather than that imposed upon us by the world.

CHINE MCDONALD

THURSDAY 21 SEPTEMBER   **JOHN 6:35–36**

Our daily bread

'I am the bread of life. Whoever comes to me will never go hungry, and whoever believes in me will never be thirsty. But as I told you, you have seen me and still you do not believe.' (NIV)

Did you know there are more than 100 different types of bread? The most consumed foodstuff in the world, it forms a central part of the diet in many countries. What English breakfast would be complete without a slice of buttery toast? What a lovely addition naan bread makes to a curry. Bagels form a key part of Jewish cuisine, while focaccia is a staple in Italy.

Bread is such a fundamental part of human community, and this is why Jesus uses this metaphor when describing himself. This would hardly resonate with the whole of humanity if he had chosen chocolate, broccoli or potatoes, would it? Of course, this is not the only mention of bread in the Bible. In the Old Testament, God sends the Jews manna from heaven during the exodus from Egypt after all the food they had brought with them had run out.

In Matthew's account of Jesus in the wilderness and his temptation by the devil, we are told that Christ's response when the devil mockingly urges him to turn stones into bread is: 'It is written: "Man shall not live on bread alone, but on every word that comes from the mouth of God."'

What Jesus is saying in today's passage is that we can live by *him* alone. He is the bread of life. He is everything that we need to have life in all its fullness. What Christ is telling us here is that we need him more than we need anything else. He is the one that we should crave every day. He is the one without whom we feel dissatisfied. He is the one who fills that gnawing sense of hunger that cannot be satisfied by anything else.

Lord, there is one thing that we would ask—that we would dwell in your house, and feast on you, the bread of life, for ever.

CHINE MCDONALD

FRIDAY 22 SEPTEMBER   **JOHN 10:7–14**

A shepherd's sacrifice

'I am the good shepherd. The good shepherd lays down his life for the sheep.' (NIV)

How many shepherds have you met? Maybe it's because I'm a city girl, but I don't recall having met any. With more than 100 mentions of shepherds in the Bible and sheep having more than 500 appearances in the Old Testament and the New Testament, is it any wonder that I associate both sheep and their shepherds with Scripture? Those hearing Jesus' words in John 10 would have been familiar with the relationship between sheep and their shepherds. They would have been aware of the dedication that shepherds had to their sheep. Often, once the shepherds had herded their sheep into the sheepfold—which was made up of four high stone walls, a door and no roof—they would lie across the doorway to keep the sheep in but also to keep intruders out.

As those listening to Jesus' words were familiar with shepherding, they would also have known that shepherds were social and religious outcasts. They may have been puzzled by Jesus likening himself to them. Shepherds were rough, rowdy, uneducated: they were seen as unclean because of the work that they did so could not take part in religious ritual or ceremonies in the temple.

Why would Jesus choose to describe himself as a good shepherd, considering their tainted reputations? We only need look at the gospel accounts to realise that Jesus did not do the expected, nor did he associate with those we might expect him to. However, regardless of the reputation they had, people would have been well aware of the dedication that shepherds had to their flocks, the love that they had for them.

In the same way that shepherds are prepared to sacrifice themselves for their sheep, Christ sacrifices himself for us, his flock, in the cosmic act of atonement.

Thank you, Lord, for laying down your life for me.

CHINE MCDONALD

SATURDAY 23 SEPTEMBER   **MATTHEW 28:16–20**

An impossible task

'And surely I am with you always, to the very end of the age.' (NIV)

I cannot begin to imagine the range of emotions that were going through the eleven disciples' minds as they stood with Jesus on the mountain in Galilee. Disappointment, fear, anxiety, joy, euphoria, apprehension, love, doubt, hope?

So much had gone before, which had brought them to this moment. Three years of following this man around and seeing the crazy, wonderful, beautiful things that he had done. They had witnessed others fall before his feet, they had watched as demons fled and blind men saw, lame men walked, people were raised from the dead and storms calmed simply by the words that came from his mouth. They had been called by him, had dropped everything to follow him. They had never quite fully 'got' him but yet they loved him. And always he was with them. Then they had watched him die—their greatest hopes and dreams crushed as he was crucified. They had thought it was all over. And yet. They had seen the risen one and he had become, before their very eyes, far greater than they had ever dared to dream.

And here they were together and he was telling them that he would be leaving them again. But he was giving them a job to do—'to make disciples of all nations'. It would probably have seemed an impossible task. But here's where he gives them a bit of hope—he tells them that he will be with them. I love how the word 'surely' is popped in just before that promise. It is an emphasis on the truth of his vow. So no matter how daunting it may feel, no matter how often they might think 'I just can't do this', they are to remember his promise.

God, thank you that you are with us. Thank you that you have not abandoned us, but remain by our side through every moment of our lives.

CHINE MCDONALD

Prayer

Catherine Butcher writes:

When I was researching the background to Edith Cavell's life for a biography to mark the centenary of her execution, I was struck afresh by the power of the Psalms.

In an effort to discover the faith that undergirded Edith's life, the faith which gave her confidence in the face of death, I used the Anglican lectionary readings for each day, which always include a Psalm.

Most Psalms include praise to God and, when read daily, they provide a positive drum-beat to everyday life, focusing on God's loving kindness, his strength and his forgiveness among his many other attributes.

As a child Edith Cavell grew up in a vicarage with her father leading the family daily in morning and evening prayer. As an adult, she trained as a nurse in an era when morning and evening prayers were said in every hospital ward. She would have said or heard a psalm almost every day of her life. When she was in prison, in solitary confinement before her execution, it was her prayer book that she asked for, and *The Imitation of Christ* by Thomas à Kempis.

The Psalms taught Edith, and teach us, much about prayer. When Jesus taught his disciples to pray, many of the prayers they already knew would have been drawn from Psalms. Today, many of us know the words of the Lord's Prayer by heart. We might say it daily, or use it as a structure for a more extended extempore prayer time, using each phrase to spark further prayers of our own.

For the next two weeks we will be using the prayer Jesus taught us as a template for a journey in prayer with the Psalms. Most of the Psalms are prayers. They express raw emotions and heartfelt praise. They point us to God's greatness, the wonder of his creation, God's character, his forgiveness and the blessing we can experience as we focus on him.

As we use the Psalms to reflect on the phrases of the Lord's Prayer, I trust that you will find a fresh perspective on the issues you face in life, and renewed trust in our wonderful heavenly Father.

SUNDAY 24 SEPTEMBER PSALM 68

Our loving Father

A father to the fatherless, a defender of widows, is God in his holy dwelling. God sets the lonely in families, he leads out the prisoners with singing. (NIV)

When Steve was seven, his dad left home and never returned. Steve tried to fill the gaping hole his father had left—first with sport, then with partying and drugs. By the time he was 18 Steve was in prison. He'd tried to fund a lavish lifestyle by smuggling drugs and was caught. Prison gave him time to think. On his release he went to church and responded to the gospel. Walking to the front he said he felt 'wave after wave of God's unconditional affirming love'; a one-time choirboy, the prodigal had returned.

When Jesus teaches us to pray he starts in the most personal way possible. He invites us to call his Father our Father. Our status as sons and daughters of God is established as the basis for everything we pray.

The psalmist knows this loving father. He knows that God can be terrifying to his enemies, but he also knows that those who are put right with God—the righteous—find him to be a father full of love. Orphans, widows, the poor and even ex-prisoners like Steve can find all their needs met in our heavenly Father's embrace. He bears our burdens and, in Christ, we receive the gift of life.

As you read this Psalm imagine yourself joining this amazing procession into the presence of God (vv. 24–27) with the singers, musicians and dancers. Because of Jesus we can come into God's presence with confidence. What issues will you bring to your Father asking: 'Summon your power, God; show us your strength…' (v. 28)?

As you use the Psalms to pray, imagine your heavenly Father, like the prodigal's father, with his arms out to receive you.

CATHERINE BUTCHER

MONDAY 25 SEPTEMBER   **PSALM 19**

Our heavenly Father

The heavens declare the glory of God; the skies proclaim the work of his hands. (NIV)

Professor David Wilkinson is an astrophysicist and academic as well as being a Methodist minister and the Principal of St John's College, Durham, where he is also a professor in the Department of Theology and Religion. Professor Wilkinson, more than most, knows the first verse of this Psalm to be true. 'The God who creates this universe with a hundred billion stars in each of a hundred billion galaxies is big enough for me to try to struggle with as a concept,' he says. His studies of the universe, its awe-inspiring nature, the elegance of the physical laws fill him with wonder but, he says, 'My knowledge and experience of God comes from the fact that I believe that God is a revealing God and that revelation comes in Jesus.'

When Jesus teaches us to pray 'Our Father in heaven' he is contrasting the intimacy of our relationship with God with the awesome reality of God, creator of the universe and all we see around us in the natural world. For David, the psalmist, God's creation and his word both reveal God's greatness. Awed by God, David asks for God's help to live a life that pleases the Lord. He recognises that God is like a rock to stand on and that he is the Redeemer, who rescues us.

Let us use this Psalm to praise God for his intimate love and to reflect on the power of his word, and particularly his word made flesh in Jesus, who shows us what God is like.

Lord, we praise you that you are the God of both power and love. Help us to please you.

CATHERINE BUTCHER

Hallowed be your name

Lord, our Lord, how majestic is your name in all the earth! You have set your glory in the heavens. (NIV)

Our language seems so limited when we honour God's name. Like the psalmist, we can make comparisons with things God has made. But we can't do him justice. *The Message* version of the Psalm helps here. Eugene Peterson translates verse 2 as 'Nursing infants gurgle choruses about you; toddlers shout the songs…'.

Toddlers aren't great orators. Their powers of description don't amount to much, but their delight can be infectious. As adults we are thrilled with every attempt by the toddlers we love to communicate with us. So it is with our Father in heaven. Jesus invites us to come to him like little children (Matthew 18:3). Our praise and worship might not be eloquent, but they delight our heavenly Father's heart.

The psalmist is astonished by God's creation, but even more so by the value God places on us, his children. Amazingly, God has even given us responsibilities to care for the earth he has created. This Psalm also looks forward to Jesus. Paul quotes from it in 1 Corinthians 15, referring to 'Christ' as 'the firstfruits of those who have fallen asleep' (v. 20). One day even death will be 'under his feet' (v. 27) and 'in Christ all will be made alive' (v. 22).

Use this Psalm and all your senses to praise God for who he is. Thank him for the natural world around you—the things you can touch, see, taste, smell and hear. If you can, learn these nine verses by heart, or read them in several translations to allow yourself to be filled with awe and wonder when you read and think about our heavenly Father.

We pray: How majestic is your name, O Lord.

CATHERINE BUTCHER

Your kingdom come

The Lord has established his throne in heaven, and his kingdom rules over all. (NIV)

When we follow Jesus in praying 'your kingdom come' what are we asking for? Matthew's Gospel in the New International Version includes 54 references to the 'kingdom'. From the very beginning of his ministry Jesus preached, 'Repent, for the kingdom of heaven has come near' (Matthew 4:17). And the phrase 'the kingdom of heaven has come near' is repeated several times in Matthew's Gospel. The kingdom Jesus is referring to is not 'pie in the sky when you die' but something much more immediate.

In Psalm 103 David summarises some of the aspects of God's kingdom—he lists the benefits in verses 3–6: all our sins forgiven; diseases healed; our lives set free from death; crowning us with love and compassion; desires satisfied; life renewed, and righteousness and justice given for all the oppressed.

When you feel low, read this psalm and give thanks for all that God has done for us in Christ. And when you pray 'your kingdom come', remember that the kingdom Jesus came to establish begins now and continues into eternity. Now we see glimpses; in eternity when God's kingdom comes we'll see it in all its fullness: 'There will be no more death or mourning or crying or pain' (Revelation 21:4). David's full list of kingdom benefits will be a reality.

In 2016 the Archbishops of Canterbury and York invited Christians to pray 'Your Kingdom Come' from Ascension Day to Pentecost, and the response was a huge wave of prayer. This year the Presidents of Churches Together with the Archbishops repeated the invitation globally. Let's continue to pray, 'Your kingdom come' and to use David's list of benefits as we pray for those we know and love who are not yet citizens of God's heavenly kingdom.

Thank you, Lord, for inviting us to join in your work of bringing others into your kingdom.

CATHERINE BUTCHER

THURSDAY 28 SEPTEMBER   **PSALM 1**

Your will be done on earth

Blessed is the one who does not walk in step with the wicked or stand in the way that sinners take or sit in the company of mockers, but whose delight is in the law of the Lord, and who meditates on his law day and night. (NIV)

There is an eternal perspective to this Psalm. When we are doing God's will, fulfilling his purpose, bringing glory to him, our lives are fruitful and prosper. We bear fruit, simply by abiding in God. Jesus has this fruitfulness in mind when he says: 'If you remain in me and I in you, you will bear much fruit' (John 15:5). This is what it is like when God's will is done on earth: the Holy Spirit produces fruit (Galatians 5:22–23), which goes much deeper than external comfort and prosperity.

In 1983 Mehdi Dibaj was arrested in Iran and spent nearly ten years in the notorious Evin prison. A fellow inmate wrote of his prison encounter with Mehdi: 'I noticed him because he was walking as a person who was very satisfied and content… I asked him, "Why are you so joyful?" He said, "I am praying to God that has made this beautiful day possible for me… I am thankful to God."' The fruit of God's Holy Spirit was evident in Mehdi's life. Later, facing the court that would sentence him to death, Medhi said: 'I would rather have the whole world against me, but know the Almighty God is with me; I may be called an apostate, but I know I have the approval of the God of glory.'

External circumstances are not a true indicator of the fruitful, prosperous life. Rather, it is the peaceful and joyful life that can face every circumstance confident of God's love. For now we look forward to eternity when the full picture of this Psalm will be restored, as John described in his picture of heaven (Revelation 22).

Take this Psalm to heart, asking God to help you draw on 'streams of living water' as you pray 'your will be done on earth'.

CATHERINE BUTCHER

FRIDAY 29 SEPTEMBER — PSALM 126

God's will as it is done in heaven

Our mouths were filled with laughter, our tongues with songs of joy. Then it was said among the nations, 'The Lord has done great things for them.' (NIV)

John's face seemed different. Before, his eyes had seemed dull; his demeanour dismissive. Now he seemed to sparkle. He said it was as if he had fallen in love for the first time. John was struggling to find words to explain that he had become a Christian. Over a period of about a week, he had discovered that Jesus is real, and had died to set us free and to give us a brand new life with him.

This Psalm has three contexts, which help us to grasp the joy of heaven. It is thought that it was written to celebrate the Israelites' return from 70 years in exile in Babylon. They celebrated for seven days as 'the Lord had filled them with joy' (Ezra 6:22). Their new-found freedom was a testimony to God's power. It was God who had changed the attitude of the king of Assyria.

A second context in which to apply the Psalm is our own deliverance from sin. Like John, as we discover that by God's grace and power we are set free from sin, we are filled with joy. This joy is often evident on the faces of those who have discovered Jesus' love and forgiveness for the first time.

Our heavenly future is the third context. When Jesus teaches us to pray, we start by acknowledging that God is in heaven, and then we ask him to change our world so that it becomes like his heavenly home; so that our reality is aligned with God's reality. One day, with him in heaven, we will see him face to face. Our joy will be complete.

Use this Psalm to thank God for all he has done for you and to consider the full joy ahead—as it is in heaven in God's presence.

CATHERINE BUTCHER

SATURDAY 30 SEPTEMBER   **PSALM 104**

Give us today our daily bread

All creatures look to you to give them their food at the proper time. When you give it to them, they gather it up; when you open your hand, they are satisfied with good things.(NIV)

Sister Maria Lourdes lives in East Timor at the tip of the Indonesian archipelago. The country gained independence in 2002 after decades of fighting. Thousands of people died as Indonesian-backed militias opposed to independence launched a scorched-earth campaign. Sister Maria was one of those who fought back with a message of love and reconciliation. When the fighting in East Timor was at its worst, 15,000 people left the city and found refuge in the forest around her house. 'God worked a miracle', she said. 'We did not have enough food for even 15 people, let alone 15,000. But each day I got up, I prayed, and then I started cooking rice—and the barrel of rice never ran out for three weeks. The day it ran out was the day the international peacekeepers came.'

God not only creates, but he sustains his creation. As we pray, 'Give us today our daily bread' we are asking our creating and sustaining God to provide for us as this Psalm describes (vv. 14–15). For Sister Maria, God answered this prayer in a miraculous way.

The Psalm uses vivid metaphors to describe how God shaped our world, with each day of creation described. Spend a few minutes comparing Genesis 1 with this Psalm to see God's creation unfolding:

- Day one: light (Genesis 1:3–5; Psalm 104:2)
- Day two: sea and sky (Genesis 1:6–8; Psalm 104:3)
- Day three: land and plants (Genesis 1:9–13; Psalm 104:5–18)
- Day four: sun, moon and stars (Genesis 1:14–19; Psalm 104:19–23)
- Day five: fish and birds (Genesis 1:20–23; Psalm 104:24–26)
- Day six: animals and people (Genesis 1:24–31; Psalm 104:24, 27–30)

What an amazing creation—and an even more amazing Creator!

Ask God to meet your needs today. Remember Jesus tells us: 'Do not worry about your life, what you will eat or drink… seek first his kingdom and his righteousness' (Matthew 6:25–34).

CATHERINE BUTCHER

Forgive our sins

If you, Lord, kept a record of sins, Lord, who could stand? But with you there is forgiveness. (NIV)

Once he became a Christian, John, whose story we read two days ago, said 'I used to think I was a good man!' In his journey to faith, he realised that he wasn't 'good' at all, but because of Jesus, he now had hope and a future (Jeremiah 29:11). Like the apostle Paul, we all need to realise that we have sinned and fall short of God's standard (Romans 3:23). The consequence of sin is death, but God gives us a free gift: forgiveness, which leads to eternal life in Christ (Romans 6:23). We can be confident that if we belong to Christ Jesus, we won't be punished for our sin. 'The Holy Spirit will give you life that comes from Christ Jesus and will set you free from sin and death' (Romans 8:1–2, CEV).

Although this Psalm was written hundreds of years before Jesus was born, the psalmist recognises that God is loving and forgiving. The author of Hebrews compares the Old Testament sacrificial system, which was designed to atone for sin, with the forgiveness Jesus gives: 'Christ went once for all into the most holy place and freed us from sin forever. He did this by offering his own blood instead of the blood of goats and bulls' (Hebrews 9:12, CEV).

As you come to God in prayer today, use this psalm to ask God to forgive any sin you have become aware of. You can be confident that he will set you free. You might like to put your name instead of 'Israel' in verse 7 as you remind yourself to 'put your hope in the Lord'.

I am sorry, Lord. Forgive me my sins.

CATHERINE BUTCHER

MONDAY 2 OCTOBER — **PSALM 32**

As we forgive...

Count yourself lucky, how happy you must be—you get a fresh start, your slate's wiped clean. (*The Message*)

According to the Mayo Clinic, a leading medical research group in the United States, 'If you don't practise forgiveness, you might be the one who pays most dearly.' The clinic points to the significant health benefits of forgiving someone, including lower blood pressure, fewer symptoms of depression, a stronger immune system, and higher self-esteem.

This Psalm points to the physical symptoms of being unforgiven (v. 3). Just as we can become depressed when we feel guilty, we can become physically unwell if we hold on to grudges, anger and unforgiveness.

The consequences of forgiveness are joy and gladness (v. 11). We can experience these positive emotions when we are forgiven by God. In turn Jesus calls us to forgive others, setting them free. To emphasise this point Jesus told the parable of the unmerciful servant (Matthew 18:21–35). Peter, the disciple, had asked Jesus, 'Lord, how many times shall I forgive my brother or sister who sins against me?' (18:21). Jesus told the story of a servant whose master had cancelled his debts. But the servant then had a fellow servant thrown into prison when he could not repay what he owed. Jesus ends the story with the challenge: 'forgive your brother or sister from your heart' (v. 35).

Read this Psalm though slowly, asking God to bring to mind any sin you have committed which needs his forgiveness. Then read it again, allowing God to show you if there is anyone you need to forgive. Just as Jesus wipes the slate clean for you, ask God for his grace to forgive others. Don't hide behind walls of self-protection built from bitterness and unforgiveness. Instead, forgive others as you have been forgiven, and take refuge in the safety of God's love.

Let God's loving arms surround you and protect you as you trust in him.

CATHERINE BUTCHER

TUESDAY 3 OCTOBER PSALM 5

Lead us not into temptation

You do what is right, and I ask you to guide me. Make your teaching clear. (CEV)

When I was single and in my 20s, God used a dream to direct me. It had never happened before, or since, but I'm so grateful for that dream. I'd been getting to know a young man who was fairly new to our church. I was enjoying his attention and friendship. I was praying about the growing relationship. Jesus taught us to pray, 'Lead me not into temptation...' and I wanted God to guide me.

One night I had a dream. I don't remember much about it, but I woke suddenly—wide awake—and knew instantly that the friendship should go no further. A few weeks later I discovered that the young man was married but had left his wife, the mother of his child, and had lied to avoid saying anything about them as I got to know him. I felt that God had saved me from embarking on a painful relationship.

This Psalm expresses some of what I felt. God hates lies. He also promises to lead us if we trust him: 'Trust in the Lord with all your heart and lean not on your own understanding; in all your ways submit to him, and he will make your paths straight' (Proverbs 3:5–6).

Jesus' guide to prayer includes this request to keep us from being tempted. The prophet Jeremiah reminds us, 'Blessed is the one who trusts in the Lord, whose confidence is in him' (Jeremiah 17:7). But he also points out that 'the heart is deceitful above all things' (Jeremiah 17:9). We need to keep asking God to lead us and guide us. He knows our hearts and, as this Psalm says, he will protect us when our hearts are set to follow his direction.

Lord, I want to follow you. Help me to hear your guiding voice.

CATHERINE BUTCHER

Deliver us from evil

Let those who love the Lord hate evil, for he guards the lives of his faithful ones and delivers them from the hand of the wicked. (NIV)

Sometimes we give evil more recognition than it deserves. In doing so we give the enemy room to bring us down. This Psalm is a useful reminder of what to do when we pray 'deliver us from evil'. The fact of the matter is 'The Lord reigns.' Our response is to be glad and rejoice, focusing on God's strength and not on evil or our own weakness.

When we dwell on evil, its power and impact in our lives grows as we devote emotional energy to thinking about it. As we focus on evil we can feel weak and defenceless. We are deceived into feeling vulnerable—when, in fact, we have God on our side. Evils of all kinds, which seem to take on mountainous proportions, 'melt like wax before the Lord' as the psalmist says (v. 5).

Praise and rejoicing are the defence mechanisms that this Psalm recommends. God showed King Jehoshaphat how this defence worked against an enemy (2 Chronicles 20:21–22). Jehoshaphat appointed men to sing to the Lord and to praise him at the head of the army. As a result their enemy was defeated. Similar tactics work in our own lives.

Once I was facing a very difficult work situation. The more I tried to tackle it, the more overwhelmed I became. I didn't know what to do, so instead of spending the journey to work fretting, I decided to listen to worship music, which reminded me of God's greatness. It was another three months before anything changed, then suddenly a new job came up, I applied and was appointed. The experience showed me the power of praise to deliver me from the power of evil.

Use this Psalm to praise God and get a new perspective on the issues in life that trouble you.

CATHERINE BUTCHER

THURSDAY 5 OCTOBER   **PSALM 145**

Yours is the kingdom

Your kingdom is an everlasting kingdom, and your dominion endures through all generations. (NIV)

Two Gospels record Jesus teaching the disciples to pray. Matthew ends the prayer with the request: 'deliver us from the evil one' (Matthew 6:13). Luke's version is shorter, ending with 'lead us not into temptation' (Luke 11:4). In the Protestant tradition a doxology—a short hymn of praise to God—is often added at the end of the Lord's Prayer: 'For the kingdom, the power, and the glory are yours, now and for ever, Amen.'

We will end this short focus on the Lord's Prayer with three Psalms of praise—tools to use in our daily lives as we keep our focus on God. In today's Psalm, David's heart is full to bursting with praise to God as he writes. He crafts each sentence carefully as an acrostic poem; the verses each begin with the successive letters of the Hebrew alphabet. The focus is on God's greatness and power that endure through all generations, prompting joyful praise and celebration. The psalmist praises God that even 'when someone stumbles or falls, you give a helping hand' (v. 14, CEV). The antidote to life's low points is to remember what God has done in the past and to recall his promises.

At this time of year we often celebrate harvest, giving thanks to God for the way he provides for our needs. Verses 15–19 point to God's goodness as our provider and protector.

Will you take time today to thank God for his work in your life? And, looking particularly at verse 4, is there someone you can tell about what God has done for you?

Could you go through the whole alphabet, thanking God for something or someone for each letter?

CATHERINE BUTCHER

FRIDAY 6 OCTOBER   **PSALM 147**

Yours is the power

Great is our Lord and mighty in power; his understanding has no limit. (NIV)

Praising God puts our lives into perspective. Our knowledge and understanding are limited, whereas our God sees 'the end from the beginning' as the prophet Isaiah records (Isaiah 46:10). That infinite knowledge goes hand in hand with God's compassion. As this Psalm reminds us, he 'renews our hopes and heals our bodies' (v. 3, CEV). Praising God helps when we are broken-hearted.

Many of the psalms start with raw emotion and pain. Psalms 42 and 43 both include the question: 'Why, my soul, are you downcast? Why so disturbed within me?' The instruction which follows is: 'Put your hope in God'; and the conclusion: 'for I will yet praise him, my Saviour and my God'. The psalms help us to refocus our thoughts away from ourselves and towards our God, who has the power to change lives and situations and the wisdom to act appropriately.

So, like many other psalms, Psalm 147 points to God's power in the natural world, which we can see. Vivid images remind us that even the snow and hail fall at his command. We are also reminded that God is not impressed by human strength—in those days an army's strength was determined by the number of foot soldiers and horses. God looks for men and women with humble hearts who trust him completely.

Finally we are reminded that God revealed his written law to his chosen people. Those of us in Christ have been adopted into this special relationship and God has given us a new covenant (Jeremiah 31:31–34) written on our hearts, for which we owe him eternal praise.

Use this Psalm to focus on God's power, to praise him and to draw on his strength.

CATHERINE BUTCHER

SATURDAY 7 OCTOBER
PSALM 149

Yours is the glory

The Lord is pleased with his people, and he gives victory to those who are humble. All of you faithful people, praise our glorious Lord! (CEV)

Although God's glory is not directly mentioned in the prayer Jesus taught his disciples, it is an appropriate ending to the doxology ('For the kingdom, the power and the *glory* are yours') which is usually added when we say the Lord's Prayer. God's glory is also an appropriate end to our fortnight in the Psalms, as it is an important theme in Jesus' prayer for us in John 17. He tells his heavenly Father, 'I have given them the *glory* that you gave me' (v. 22, NIV). The impact of God's glory in us is unity with a purpose: so that the world will know that Jesus is sent by God on a mission of love (v. 23).

Jesus tells his Father 'I want those you have given me to be with me where I am, and to see my glory' (John 17:24, NIV). He wants us to be part of the self-emptying, loving relationship, which characterises the unity of God the Father, Son and Holy Spirit.

Today's Psalm is one of victory. It suggests the different ways in which we can praise and delight in the God of glory, and shows that this is a two-way relationship. God delights in us. Jesus' prayer is being answered when we are caught up in praise to our glorious heavenly Father.

The double-edged sword the psalmist refers to looks forward to the final victory parade of heaven and to John's vision of Christ: 'like a son of man dressed in a robe reaching down to his feet and with a golden sash round his chest' (Revelation 1:13–16, NIV). The sharp, double-edged sword, which is also mentioned in Hebrews 4:12–14, speaks of the judgement Jesus will exercise at the end of time. To him be the glory.

Let's take this Psalm to heart and 'praise our glorious Lord!'—who enjoys our worship and is preparing a place for us to be with him, enjoying his presence for ever.

CATHERINE BUTCHER

Confidence

Anne Calver writes:

When I reflect on my personal journey with the Lord I am deeply conscious of requiring boldness. We need confidence for so many different aspects of our lives—for stepping out, for overcoming hurdles, for seizing the moment and for coming out of the shadows. My heart's cry, as you read the following passages and consider the biblical characters, is that their confidence will increase yours; not because they are good role models, but because you are hungry to do whatever it takes to see Christ's kingdom come, and his will be done on earth as it is in heaven.

The overriding realisation that I have had whilst studying these passages is that we do not have to manufacture confidence but that when we ask the Holy Spirit to come and fill us and equip us to serve God, we will find strength that we never knew we had. You can be like the woman at the well who evangelised her town; but only if you drink the living water. You can speak up with confidence and anointing like Peter, but only if the Spirit empowers you. We can set about doing all kinds of jobs and activities in our own strength (and they may even gain human recognition) but true boldness that transforms lives for eternity can only be found in the power of Jesus.

When Peter stands on the edge of the boat and looks out, he witnesses the king of the world walking on water. The other disciples see Jesus too, but they are gripped with fear. Instead of letting fear dictate his decision, Peter chooses a different path by saying to his master, 'Lord if it is you, tell me to come to you on the water' (Matthew 14:22–33). Jesus replies to his son, 'Come.' We choose whether to join Jesus on the water, to get out of our comfort zones and be bold for him, and if we do, we can guarantee that we will witness the Lord do wonderful things.

As you read the following reflections, my prayer is that your heart will be open enough to say to Jesus: 'If you are asking me to do this, I will.' May your risk-taking grow and thus your confidence increase so that you change your bit of the world in Jesus' name. Amen!

SUNDAY 8 OCTOBER ACTS 2:14–24

Confidence in speaking up

Then Peter stood up with the Eleven, raised his voice and addressed the crowd: 'Fellow Jews and all of you who live in Jerusalem, let me explain this to you; listen carefully to what I say.' (NIV)

This passage comes immediately after the disciples have been filled with the Spirit. Before they receive the Spirit, the believers have been constantly gathering together, talking, praying and waiting for the Lord, fearfully wondering what was going to happen. Just as the disciples gathered in John 20:19 before they saw the risen Lord, here the disciples gather just before they receive the Holy Spirit. Suddenly we witness a huge change in these followers of Christ—no longer are they hiding, no longer wondering what is about to happen. Instead they are filled with boldness to speak up and proclaim the truth about the Messiah. The power of the Holy Spirit has touched Peter in such a way that he confidently speaks up and declares to the crowd who Jesus is and what they are witnessing. He has no idea how they will respond to him but he does not care; Peter is filled with the Spirit and knows that he has to share the reality of what is happening.

I wonder how many of us lack confidence in sharing the truth of what we believe. I wonder how often we forget that the power of the Holy Spirit can give us boldness to speak out and find the right words to talk about Jesus. It is so easy to hide away and pray in places where no one is looking but so challenging to put aside what people may think of us and speak up anyway. Confidence grows as we begin to speak up—we may not have all the words initially, but we can trust that they will come as we step out in faith. Don't let fear stop you sharing Jesus; who knows whose life he may wish to transform today through you?

Are you entering a situation today where the Lord may be calling you to speak up confidently about his work in your life? Ask the Holy Spirit to fill you and guide you afresh.

ANNE CALVER

MONDAY 9 OCTOBER   **JOHN 4:25–42**

Confidence in stepping out

Then, leaving her water jar, the woman went back to the town and said to the people, 'Come, see a man who told me everything I've ever done. Could this be the Messiah?' They came out of the town and made their way towards him. (NIV)

I love this story of the woman at the well—how her life is completely transformed after encountering Jesus. She is so affected by what he tells her about who she is and who he is, that she has to go and tell her town. You can imagine her tossing her water jar to one side and running across the field back to her people—she knows that taking the water from the well to them will not give them life in the way that the living water can. There is a sense of her being compelled to share the good news that she has just discovered, and she knows that it can change every life for ever. Later in the passage we hear how powerful the woman's words have been: 'Many of the Samaritans from that town believed in him because of the woman's testimony, "He told me everything I've ever done"' (4:39).

This is a woman who would not have felt confident. We know that it was a time of day that women would not have been drawing water from the well and yet here she was; alone, a woman cast out because of her behaviour—a woman who had no doubt caused a lot of pain to other people. However, Jesus transforms her life to such an extent that she is filled with confidence to step out and ignore what people would think of her, and run and bring them to Jesus. This woman doesn't know if she will be heard but she takes a risk and goes to share the gospel anyway. Wow! How many of us need to lay down what people may think of us or what they have planned for us, and take a risk in stepping out with Jesus.

Lord Jesus, please give us courage to step out like the woman at the well. Enable us to remember what you have saved us from, giving us a renewed hunger and faith to tell our friends and neighbours.

ANNE CALVER

TUESDAY 10 OCTOBER   **ESTHER 4:12–17; 7:1–4**

Confidence in the moment

'For if you remain silent at this time, relief and deliverance for the Jews will arise from another place, but you and your father's family will perish. And who knows but that you have come to your royal position for such a time as this?' (NIV)

Strong and direct words are reported to Esther from Mordecai her cousin or 'father' (2:7). Mordecai is clearly a wise man and Esther takes his advice at every turn (2:10, 20). However, now is the time when Esther has to rise up. She cannot rely on her family to speak for her or to act on her behalf. Esther is the one who is in the position for the Lord to use her; she is the one capable of making a difference if she can find the confidence to do it.

Thankfully she does go to the king on behalf of the Jews, in order to try and save them. She does not go immediately into his presence but spends three days asking others to join with her in fasting and praying. All the wisdom that she has received from Mordecai is now released through her. Bit by bit Esther woos the king, watches and waits for the right moment and brings her case before him, until in chapter 7 the queen stands up and confidently says, 'Spare my people.'

Sometimes the Lord wants us to recognise the position and place that he has put us in and ask the question; 'Are we here for such a time as this?' Our fear, weakness and insecurities can cloud our vision of what Jesus may want to do through us and so we continue life in the same way. God may be calling you to step out and say or do something risky, which may not be received well, but we can trust that he will be with us. Only fools rush in, but perhaps it is time to fast and pray over a situation that needs your attention and then ask for wisdom and confidence to know how to act.

What position or place do you find yourself where there are very few people who have faith in Jesus? How can you use this situation for his glory?

ANNE CALVER

WEDNESDAY 11 OCTOBER   **ACTS 9:1–19**

Confidence in the calling

The Lord told him, 'Go to the house of Judas on Straight Street and ask for a man from Tarsus named Saul, for he is praying. In a vision he has seen a man named Ananias come and place his hands on him to restore his sight.' (NIV)

This is an unbelievably challenging situation! A man called Saul is breathing out murderous threats to the believers and throwing them into prison, and yet here we see the Lord calling Ananias to go to the man and heal him! Can you imagine what is running through his head? I would be thinking, 'Are you kidding me, Lord? I don't believe you! Surely I have heard that wrong?' And, yes, Ananias does question Jesus at first but then he goes to the house on Straight Street, enters it, places his hands on Saul, heals him and then baptises him.

    I think it would have been so easy just to send a message via someone to say 'God wants to heal and use you' or to shout a message through the door and then turn and run as fast as his legs would carry him, but no, Ananias is obedient to all the Lord is asking him to do.

    Jesus is not in the business of wanting us to cut corners and tell half-truths. He longs for us to hear the full extent of his call—whether in the big picture or the small—and be willing to walk confidently into every part of it. It will be scary, there will be uncertainty over some of it and you can guarantee that sometimes what we do in his name will seem crazy to people, but we can trust that the Lord is working to carry out his kingdom purposes through us.

'Immediately, something like scales fell from Saul's eyes, and he could see again' (9:18). Let's pray that the Spirit of the living God will enable us to see what he sees and hear him when he calls.

ANNE CALVER

THURSDAY 12 OCTOBER **1 SAMUEL 17:32–51**

Confidence in adversity

'All those gathered here will know that it is not by sword or spear that the Lord saves; for the battle is the Lord's, and he will give all of you into our hands.' (NIV)

If we put ourselves into the sandals of the characters in the story we begin to see a different perspective from our own. Looking through David's eyes as we read these verses, they reveal a shepherd boy who saw things differently from the rest of his people. Where everyone else seemed to see a mountain that was impossible to climb or—literally—a giant that could not be defeated, David saw a molehill, and an ant that could easily be crushed. The perspective of this boy is totally astonishing and appealing. If he could see Goliath in this way then he could go on to scale some incredible heights—and we know he did.

In the face of adversity David's confidence seems to grow because he knows that by using his proven ability to kill a lion and a bear, coupled with the power of God Most High, the Israelites can be delivered from their enemy. Previously David may have been doing work that was unseen by Saul and others, but God was using every single bit of his journey to get him ready for what lay ahead. Shepherding the flock was to lead to shepherding the people and part of that process involved overcoming one (giant) obstacle after another.

I believe that the Lord longs for us to see things through his eyes; to have his perspective so that we can see mountains as molehills and overcome many challenges. In the midst of adversity we have a choice—we can lose confidence like the Israelites did, or we can believe God for the strength to overcome. David's confidence is down to his experience, his perspective and his faith.

Lord Jesus, please help us to draw on our experiences, to have a greater glimpse of your perspective and to believe in your victory when we are facing challenges.

ANNE CALVER

FRIDAY 13 OCTOBER DANIEL 3:12–30

Confidence, even in the fire

They saw that the fire had not harmed their bodies, nor was a hair of their heads singed; their robes were not scorched, and there was no smell of fire on them. (NIV)

The more I read this passage, the more amazing it seems to be: to imagine a furnace being heated seven times hotter than its normal heat—so hot that the flames of the fire kill the soldiers who are taking Shadrach, Meshach and Abednego up there (v. 22). Then they are firmly tied and thrown into the furnace, because they will not worship the image of gold that Nebuchadnezzar has set up. These three men could have been consumed with fear of the fiery death awaiting them and recanted; and yet, even if they felt terror, they stuck to their decision to be faithful to God.

Faced with what seemed inevitable death, Shadrach, Meshach and Abednego are so confident in their Lord that they boldly proclaim he can save them (v. 17). The men do not try and make excuses for their rebellion or plead to escape what lies ahead of them; they are faithful to the Lord at every turn. And he rescues them!

When we are faced with life's 'fires' it is so hard to stand strong in the Lord and walk into them, trusting that he is with us and will save us. I am sure that the prospect of imminent death would cause many of us to hide from our faith, try and run away or make excuses. When you think of all those who are being persecuted for their faith all over the world, you wonder how strong they feel in the face of it and what your own reaction would be. Jesus is calling his children to have confidence in him no matter what fires we face and to proclaim who he is and what he can do, even if we feel terrified.

What fires do you face? Are you trying to avoid them? Why not ask Jesus to fill you with fresh faith today to walk forward in confidence with him? He never leaves us.

ANNE CALVER

SATURDAY 14 OCTOBER   **MATTHEW 26:36–46**

Confidence to be real

Going a little farther, he fell with his face to the ground and prayed, 'My Father, if it is possible, may this cup be taken from me. Yet not as I will, but as you will.' (NIV)

This has to be the worst trial that anyone has ever had to face. To know that you are going to be betrayed, rejected, beaten, humiliated, flogged and sacrificed before a jeering crowd and yet that you will go through with it because of your love for them, is a pill so difficult to swallow.

It is a relief to read that Jesus was not praying, 'Lord, I willingly go to my death with all the strength I need.' To discover in this passage that the Son of God was deeply anxious and asked the Father more than once if there was another way to walk forward is somehow a deep encouragement. Even Christ struggled before the biggest trial of all time. I love the honesty of Jesus before he is arrested. He doesn't pretend that everything is OK and that he has all the confidence he needs; no, he shares his heart's cry with the Father.

I do believe that the Lord is longing for his children to be completely real with him and to speak the truth from our hearts. The trial that we face may not change, but if we meet with him in honest relationship, we find a new perspective in which we can ultimately surrender to his will. Walking through trials with the confidence that we need demands an authentic relationship with Jesus that will deepen our trust in him and his plans.

The disciples are called to 'watch and pray' (v. 41) and yet they are sleeping. The biggest event in all of history is about to happen and the disciples nearly miss it because their human weakness is taking over. This challenges us to ask, 'Are we watching and praying to see what the Lord is doing or about to do?'

'Trust in the Lord with all your heart and lean not on your own understanding; in all your ways submit to him, and he will make your paths straight' (Proverbs 3:5–6).

ANNE CALVER

SUNDAY 15 OCTOBER — GENESIS 39:1–23

Confidence in the future

But while Joseph was there in the prison, the Lord was with him; he showed him kindness and granted him favour in the eyes of the prison warder. (NIV)

Joseph was destined for great things. He was a son who was longed for and loved deeply by his parents. Joseph also had prophetic dreams and the ability to interpret them. He may have grown up filled with loving assurance; however, his life suddenly turns sour. Sold by his brothers into slavery, living in a foreign household in a strange land, accused of trying to have an affair with his master's wife, thrown into prison for two years, losing everything and everyone… how can he find a way to rise again and have hope for the future?

Somehow, Joseph does not give up. We read again and again that the Lord was with him; even though life was extremely challenging, God never left his side. The Lord does not make Joseph have a tough time, nor do these painful years steal the calling or the gifts that the Lord has put into Joseph's life. He is able to use his gift of interpreting dreams and is put in charge in Egypt—Joseph would never have planned any of this!

Would the 17-year-old dreamer that we meet in Genesis 37 have been a great leader without these trials? I doubt it. Joseph grew in intimacy with the Lord to such an extent that he was more dependent on him than on anyone else. His weakness became an opportunity to lean on God and go his way rather than to trust in his own decisions.

Your journey may have made you lose confidence in God and in your future. Whatever you have faced or are going through, he is with you and you have not lost your gifts. Jesus can use all your experiences to paint a brighter, hopeful future.

Lord Jesus, please will you give me hope for a brighter future. May my past not eat away at my present or my future with you. Lord, please use my experiences to deepen my relationship with you.

ANNE CALVER

MONDAY 16 OCTOBER   **JOHN 11:17–44**

Confidence in miracles

Jesus called in a loud voice, 'Lazarus come out!' The dead man came out, his hands and feet wrapped with strips of linen, and a cloth round his face. (NIV)

This is a truly awesome story. As Jesus raises Lazarus from the dead he proves that he truly is the Son of God. Only God can give and take away life—he most certainly is 'the resurrection and the life'. Jesus calls Lazarus from death to life, from darkness to light, from captivity to freedom. Jesus longs for his children to believe in his power to set them free. He is in the business of saving lives and changing lives, for ever. He shows us time and again just how powerful he is as he feeds thousands of people, heals the sick, drives out evil spirits and so much more.

The fact is, these miracles don't stop when Jesus ascends to the Father. He sends the promised Holy Spirit (Acts 2) and the apostles 'performed many signs and wonders among the people' (Acts 5:12). The miracles do not end when the apostles die; the powerful work of God continues.

God is calling his children to believe that more is possible, to expect greater things than those we read about. He longs that we would not get sucked into a worldly road of comfort and secularism, but press closer in and seek his face. One of my friends is in her mid-eighties and she has just started seeing angels. She keeps telling me that she has never seen angels before but reports a sense of them above the church. Another friend takes to the streets every Saturday and frequently witnesses God heal people as she lays her hands on them. Their experiences increase our expectancy of what the Lord is doing in our area and cause us to believe and pray for more.

Do you have faith to believe that the Lord Jesus wants to work miraculously through your life? There is so much more. Let's step out together in prayer and expect greater things!

ANNE CALVER

TUESDAY 17 OCTOBER MARK 5:21–43

Confidence in myself

He took her by the hand and said to her *'Talitha koum!'* (which means 'Little girl, I say to you, get up!'). Immediately the girl stood up and walked around (she was twelve years old). (NIV)

As far as the house of Jairus is concerned, the girl is dead and there is absolutely no point in bothering Jesus. From a human point of view it is all over for the girl and everyone around her has stopped believing she can live again. Her little world has fallen into darkness and the world around her is in a place of desperation. Jesus answers these cries of pain with the perplexing words: 'Don't be afraid, just believe.'

His perspective is so entirely different from ours. We may think that something is finished, we find ourselves full of fear and believing the worst and yet Jesus says these words; 'Don't be afraid—don't give up on me.'

Recently I heard the testimony of a girl whose life, from our point of view, was over. She had been taking hard drugs for a long time, her background was deeply broken, she had nothing and no hope and everyone had given up on her. Then Jesus stepped in. He turned her darkness into light and her sorrow into dancing. He gave her hope and a future (see Jeremiah 29:11).

Our life may not look like hers, but perhaps we still need to hear these words from Jesus. He is calling out to us: *'Talitha koum!'* 'Little girl, get up! Rise up and become the person I have called you to be. Do not live in the shadows of who you used to be, but step into the glorious light found in being my child.' We all have areas of our life that are asleep or feel dead within us. Maybe it is time to dream again of what could be. There is so much more for each one of us.

'For the light makes everything visible. This is why it is said: "Awake, O sleeper, rise up from the dead, and Christ will give you light"' (Ephesians 5:14, NLT).

ANNE CALVER

WEDNESDAY 18 OCTOBER   **EXODUS 4:1–17; 5:1**

Confidence in obedience

Afterwards Moses and Aaron went to Pharaoh and said, 'This is what the Lord, the God of Israel, says: "Let my people go, so that they may hold a festival to me in the wilderness."' (NIV)

When I think initially of Moses I think of a great man and a strong leader who led the Israelites towards the promised land. And yes, Moses is incredible: 'No prophet has risen in Israel like Moses, whom the Lord knew face to face, who did all those signs and wonders the Lord sent him to do in Egypt' (Deuteronomy 34:10–11). We can find ourselves focusing on how great Moses was and forget how weak he was too. We can skate over his insecurities and identity questions, looking instead to splitting the Red Sea and leading the Israelites through safely.

The reality is that Moses lacked confidence when it came to being obedient to the Lord God. In Exodus 3 and 4 the Lord tells Moses to go to Pharaoh and ask him to 'let my people go'; Moses makes it plain five times that he does not feel up to the job! He questions 'Who am I?' (3:11); 'Suppose I go…?' (3:13); 'What if they do not believe me or listen to me?' (4:1); I have never been eloquent' (4:10); and finally, 'Please send someone else' (4:13)!

Being obedient to what the Lord asks of us is really hard! I am not sure he ever meant it to be easy because if it was, why would we need God's guiding hand? The Lord does not want Moses to be full of confidence in his own ability but instead he wants him to know that he, the Lord, is with him and will help him overcome his insecurities as he moves forward.

God has rescued Moses and now he wants to use Moses to rescue his people (Exodus 3:8). Obedience is about realising what God has done in you and allowing him to release it through you.

Lord Jesus, thank you for saving me. Thank you for what you have done in my life. Please help me to be confident enough to step out in obedience, overcoming my personal hurdles.

ANNE CALVER

THURSDAY 19 OCTOBER   **MATTHEW 6:25–34**

Confidence in God's provision

'Do not worry about tomorrow, for tomorrow will worry about itself. Each day has enough trouble of its own.' (NIV)

So often I find myself thinking ahead, not just to tomorrow but the day after and possibly the week after that. Thoughts are one thing, but worrying and fretting about what is to come is so unhelpful! Every time I share my future concerns with my husband, he says: 'Anne, do not worry about tomorrow, for tomorrow will worry about itself!' It is so maddening! I cannot think of one single time where worrying has added anything or helped me with anything that is ahead of me. Oh, how we long to be like the birds of the air that are so free!

Jesus is very clear in these words in Matthew: seek first his kingdom and his righteousness and all these other things that we fret about will be sorted. If we look to love the Lord our king and serve him in the places where we are, and if we do that before anything else, then he will take care of the rest.

When we put our house on the market to move south, I was not confident in God's provision. I could believe for a house (just about) but I struggled to believe for the right job and for two school places for my children (my husband and I both fretted over this!). We did not need to! On the first day of term in a new area of the UK we had one school place, but on entering the infant school we were told that a child was not returning and our son could take his place. The Lord provided exactly the right ministry roles for us and organised everything in a way that I could never have planned!

Is there an area of your life in which you need to trust God? Perhaps he is asking you to turn your worries into prayers of trust and faith today. Remember: seek him first!

ANNE CALVER

FRIDAY 20 OCTOBER   **1 KINGS 3:16–28**

Confidence in wisdom

When all Israel heard the verdict the king had given, they held the king in awe, because they saw that he had wisdom from God to administer justice. (NIV)

Sometimes we ask God for something and it is not until some time has gone by that we realise that he has answered our prayer. Solomon had asked the Lord for 'a discerning heart… and to distinguish between right and wrong' (1 Kings 3:9). In this subsequent passage we discover that the king is exercising this gift and the people are deeply aware of it.

Solomon shows such incredible wisdom in this decision with the two mothers and the baby boy. You can imagine standing there thinking, 'What on earth shall I do in this situation?' You watch these women arguing over a tiny baby and have no clear answer about how to proceed. However, God steps in and clearly shows Solomon what to do.

We so often proceed in our own strength, relying on our limited human understanding and knowledge; subsequently finding ourselves in tight corners with a desperate need for light to shine on a situation. Sometimes I feel out of my depth in a pastoral situation and find myself trying to find a helpful way ahead for individuals. Whilst frequently praying before these conversations, I have recently felt challenged to use 'arrow prayers' in the middle of the chat. In my mind I shoot one-liners up to God: 'Lord, will you come by your Spirit and put words in my mouth' or 'Father, please help me to hear the truth here, and see what you see.' By the end of the conversation I notice that something has shifted and the person is in a better place.

God longs for his children to seek him confidently for wisdom: he can make a way when there seems to be no way.

'The mouths of the righteous utter wisdom, and their tongues speak what is just. The law of their God is in their hearts; their feet do not slip' (Psalm 37:30–31).

ANNE CALVER

SATURDAY 21 OCTOBER   **ROMANS 12:1–8**

Confidence in holiness

Therefore, I urge you, brothers and sisters, in view of God's mercy, to offer your bodies as a living sacrifice, holy and pleasing to God—this is your true and proper worship. (NIV)

Holiness can seem such an old-fashioned Old Testament word, impossible to attain. The idea of God being holy can sum up a distant, 'other' being that we cannot relate to. And yet the Lord wants us to draw near to him and to become more like hm. It is fascinating that when Isaiah comes into the presence of God he declares; 'Woe to me!... For I am a man of unclean lips' (Isaiah 6:5). The holiness of God makes Isaiah aware of his sinful nature. When we encounter God, we realise our weakness and how 'unholy' we are.

I don't know about you, but I want to know Jesus, be more like him and confidently serve him. The more I know God, the more I discover things that need to be removed from my life so that I can, like Peter, keep stepping out onto the water in confidence and obedience. Jesus reminds us that 'blessed are the pure in heart, for they will see God' (Matthew 5:8). Wow, seeing God every moment working among us and through us would be truly incredible! To be radiant like Moses (Exodus 34:29) and shine like Stephen (Acts 6:15) because of our closeness with the Lord—surely our hearts long for this?

Do you long to see God and witness him move in your neighbourhood? For this to happen we need to get on our knees in worship and prayer, seeking him above all else. Only in this place of worship and prayer can we be filled with power from on high, begin to look more like Christ and serve him with greater confidence.

Father, thank you that we can draw near to you and become more like you. Please give us the desire to be shaped into your likeness and the confidence to be set apart for you.

ANNE CALVER

God's ways and means

Jean Watson writes:

Christians often say or write things like the following: 'The Lord has been very good to me'; 'God blessed us'; 'the Lord helped me in my difficulties'; 'Jesus was with us'. It's lovely to hear or read words like these but I often want to ask, 'How and in what ways has God/Jesus/the Holy Spirit been good to you, blessed you, helped you, been with you, provided for you?' Because I really want to know other people's honest, specific answers to those questions. I want to know whether it was that they had a strong sense that God was speaking to them, providing for them, loving them. Was it as they read the Bible, or did they see a light from heaven as Paul did or had a dream as the magi did; or was it as people came and listened to them empathetically, delivered meals to them, took them to their hospital appointments; or as they listened to music, read a book, walked in the countryside, went to a quiet morning…?

I came to a point in my life when I realised that it was important to recognise and identify all the ways and means by which God helps, heals, speaks, provides, guides, blesses. And I also came to realise that identifying the ways and means doesn't diminish our perception of God's goodness, love and faithfulness: it enhances it! It tells us more about how he chooses to make his goodness real and tangible to us.

Scripture, of course, is a crucially important way in which God 'speaks' to us and in Scripture we find identified, explicitly or implicitly, God's ways and means of relating to us, revealing himself to us and encouraging our growth into wholeness of mind, body and spirit. I want to look at some of these—there are plenty of others and I hope you will be stimulated to keep looking out for them.

God relates to and communicates with us both through seemingly extraordinary things and also ordinary, everyday things; through people of all sorts with their varying skills, gifts and trainings; and through the world he created. Through expected or unexpected ways and means, God may choose to channel his messages, his healing, his provision, his love and care to us. What humility! What graciousness!

SUNDAY 22 OCTOBER   **JOB 38:4–11**

Creation

'Where were you when I laid the earth's foundation? Tell me, if you understand. Who marked off its dimensions? Surely you know!' (NIV)

You may want to read more of Job 38—41 for this astonishing and wide-ranging poetic description of God's creative activity.

Romans 1:20 says: 'Since the creation of the world God's invisible qualities—his eternal power and divine nature—have been clearly seen, being understood from what has been made, so that people are without excuse.' This verse identifies one of God's ways and means of 'speaking' to us about who he is and what he is like: creation—this whole incredible universe with all its beauty, variety, regularity and interconnectedness; with all its potential provision for our physical, intellectual, aesthetic, psychological and spiritual needs.

The verse identifies two characteristics of God that can be deduced from his creation: his eternal power and his divine nature. What aspects of the universe do you think reveal these characteristics? What other characteristics of God are implied or clearly demonstrated by the world about us? Think of what we can learn about artists from their works: not just their creative ability, but also their characters, what delights or distresses them, their values, what they want to say to others…

Jesus was very aware of the world about him. He showed his control of nature at times; he used aspects of nature for his parables—earthly stories with heavenly meanings. Being made in the image of God and following Jesus must mean enjoying and learning from creation and being in one way or another creative—the first implied characteristic of God in Scripture: in the beginning God created…

Earth's crammed with heaven,
And every common bush afire with God;
But only he who sees takes off his shoes.
Elizabeth Barrett Browning (1806–61)

Take time today—whatever the weather!—to be open to creation and to anything it might be 'telling' you about its creator and about his attitude towards all he has created, including you.

JEAN WATSON

MONDAY 23 OCTOBER   **JONAH 3:1–10**

Prophets and messengers

'Go to the great city of Nineveh and proclaim to it the message that I give you.' Jonah obeyed the word of the Lord and went to Nineveh. (NIV)

Scripture is full of some of the human ways and means by which God spoke to people. In the Old Testament particularly, it was often through the prophets—God's special messengers. I could have chosen any one of these but I want to focus on Jonah. Given a message he didn't want to deliver, to a place to which he didn't want to go, he tried to run away. (I don't think this story tells us that God always thinks of the 'work' you don't want to do and calls you to it!) However, Jonah reacted as he did and ended up in hot water; well, actually cold water, as you will know if you have read, now or previously, the whole book of Jonah.

In today's passage, God gives Jonah his message for Nineveh a second time and this time Jonah obeys. He goes to Nineveh and roundly tells the Ninevites off for their wickedness which God has seen (Jonah 1:1–2). The Ninevites repent and are forgiven and Jonah sulks. What God then says to him did, I hope, make him feel ashamed. He should have been delighted that God was merciful rather than annoyed that Nineveh hadn't been overthrown as he had been telling everyone it would be after 40 days.

What I find interesting about the biblical prophets and about people who are God's missionaries or messengers today (and shouldn't that be all of us, in different ways?) is how very different they were and we are. Yet, warts, differences and all, God chooses to pass on his messages to the world through us—whether we are leaders or lay people, through our different callings and personalities, by our words, our characters and our lives. Even through me, or you.

Do you see yourself in any sense as a prophet or messenger of God? Talk to God about your answer to this, or your uncertainty or ambivalence about it.

                                                                        JEAN WATSON

TUESDAY 24 OCTOBER   **ROMANS 13:1–6**

Leaders—those in authority

The authorities that exist have been established by God. (NIV)

Clearly, this is a statement about God's ideal—about the way things should be. However, in this flawed world, they aren't always. God's plan, according to our Romans passage, is to appoint those in authority for the good of the people. Their function is to take good care of their subjects and punish wrongdoing. History tells us that, over and over again, authority figures have abused their powers—with disastrous consequences.

Good leaders, on the other hand, can be among God's ways and means of caring for us and providing for our needs: keeping us safe, ensuring that we can live in peace, organising things for our health and well-being.

1 Samuel 16 is about God choosing one such leader—David. He wasn't perfect, but he was God's servant for the good of his people; he did try to love and obey God and improve the lot and the status and standing of his people. He was a leader under God's authority. David was one of God's ways and means of revealing himself to his people in Old Testament times; and God still uses him today wherever the Scriptures are read. Through David's life and through the psalms he wrote, and of course supremely through 'great David's greater son', Jesus, we know what God is like, what he has done and continues to do for us and what he wants of us.

What is your experience of and attitude to leaders and authority? Can you identify an occasion when someone in authority has been God's means of blessing you? In what circumstances should people in authority be obeyed and supported or resisted and called to account?

O God, whatever authority or influence I may have, may I wield it as Jesus wielded his, and so be one of your ways and means of helping and blessing others.

JEAN WATSON

WEDNESDAY 25 OCTOBER MARK 6:30–44

Followers, disciples, willing people

'You give them something to eat.' (NIV)

These words were spoken by Jesus to his disciples when they suggested he should send the crowds away to buy food for themselves. It was getting late and they were in a solitary, remote place. Jesus had compassion on the people. So how did he show that compassion? First of all, he taught them many things: he spoke truth to them from God, meeting their spiritual needs. Then the disciples made their suggestion and Jesus brought into play two other ways and means by which the people's physical needs could be met: nourishing food and willing people—the disciples and other 'ordinary' people. They organised the crowd and saw to it that the food was distributed, shared, eaten and cleared away. Of course, Jesus said the blessing and performed the miracle but the actual getting of God's provision to the people involved ordinary willing followers, like us. (Similarly today, although God is the ultimate provider of our daily food, a whole range of people are his ways and means of bringing it to us.)

When I use the word 'ordinary' to refer to people like us, I'm not using it in a derogatory sense at all; we are all 'special' to someone and to God but we're not all in positions of official leadership. Throughout the Bible God uses ordinary people in that sense to be his messengers and reflect something of his character: to teach, warn, encourage, show compassion to… one another. He still does the same today: he still exhorts us to 'love your neighbour as yourself'. I have a mental list of 'angels'—some very unexpected and unlikely ones—who have been there for me when I needed a 'neighbour'.

Think about and thank God for some 'ordinary' people who have been or are God's ways and means of blessing you in some way. How about thinking of a creative way of thanking them too?

JEAN WATSON

THURSDAY 26 OCTOBER   ACTS 16:16–31

An earthquake—and prisoners

Suddenly there was such a violent earthquake that the foundations of the prison were shaken. At once all the prison doors flew open, and everyone's chains came loose. (NIV)

At one time natural phenomena such as earthquakes and tsunamis were called acts of God and couldn't be insured against. I don't know whether this is still the case.

We have already noted that Jesus showed his control of nature—stilling a storm, walking on water.

In our passage, Paul and Silas were in Philippi. After healing a slave girl and inadvertently causing a riot, they were stripped, beaten and put in prison. The earthquake occurred while Paul and Silas were praying and singing and the other prisoners were listening. The earthquake, allowed by God, set all the prisoners physically free, but God's message through Paul and Silas was the means of setting the jailer and others spiritually free. They assured the jailer that no one had escaped and hence stopped the terrified official from killing himself. Then, when asked, they explained God's way of salvation to him.

If you read on in the story you will see that the jailer then became one of God's ways and means to take care of Paul and Silas—he washed their wounds and set a meal before them. Not long after this, the authorities apologised for having imprisoned Paul and Silas and released them, hoping they would leave the city as soon as possible.

Nature can be calm and beautiful but also, as in the earthquake of our passage, violent and destructive. Albeit beyond our comprehension, God sometimes allows it to be the latter. Mysteriously and paradoxically, he has ways and means of 'speaking' to us in, and bringing good out of, seemingly terrible and disastrous events, natural or man-made. And if we are open to listening to him and ready to be his hands and feet, we can be part of his ways and means of overcoming evil with good.

Reflect on any 'earthquakes' in your life. How do you see them and how have they affected you or are affecting you? Can you talk to God and a trusted friend/counsellor about this?

JEAN WATSON

FRIDAY 27 OCTOBER
EXODUS 35:30—36:7

People with creative gifts

So Bezalel, Oholiab and every skilled person to whom the Lord has given skill and ability to know how to carry out all the work of constructing the sanctuary are to do the work just as the Lord has commanded. (NIV)

We thought earlier about God's creativity; here we see God calling people with creative gifts to build the sanctuary and to make it very beautiful. If we read on we see that a huge variety of high-quality materials and lovely textures and colours were used in this construction. There must have been artists, silver- and goldsmiths, carpenters and many other skilled people involved.

How would you answer these questions: what was the point of making such a sanctuary? What does it tell us about God's character and about what he wanted to say to his people through the construction and appearance of the sanctuary? Do any of these suggestions ring true for you?

- If we are made in God's image, we must all have the ability in some measure to reflect something of that creativity.
- God must want us to reflect whatever creative gifts and skills he has given us to bless others and please him.
- Only the best is good enough for God.
- God delights in beauty and in creativity.
- Good art and those who use their artistic/creative/constructive skills for God are among God's ways and means of communicating with, teaching, refreshing and blessing us.

We can't all be Bezalels or Oholiabs. But we don't have to be great artists to please God and bless others, because we can be creative in any areas of our lives: in our relationships; in our hospitality; our letters and emails; in our prayer and worship. With imagination, love and effort, we can all find ways of being creative that will please God and bless others.

How can my imagination and creativity be stimulated and reflected in my life and relationships, starting with my relationship with God?

JEAN WATSON

SATURDAY 28 OCTOBER   MARK 4:1–20

Parables, stories

[Jesus] taught them many things by parables, and in his teaching said: 'Listen! A farmer went out to sow his seed.' (NIV)

In Jesus' parable, the farmer sows seed in different kinds of soil with different results. The seed stands for God's word or message. Some people don't really hear it; others receive it but don't act on it; still others act on it for a while but then are distracted by other words or messages which are not from God. Finally there are those who hear, receive, act on it and produce fruit from it in their lives.

    Even the disciples had to have this parable explained to them. So, why did Jesus often speak in parables—tell earthly stories with a heavenly, spiritual meaning? Why did he not instead spell out clearly to everyone what the message was? I haven't found any easy answers to these questions. One suggestion is that the disciples who had been with Jesus and had heard his teaching and seen his actions and attitudes were more likely to be ready to understand certain truths; more likely to have ears to hear, as Jesus put it, and so more likely to be able to discern the spiritual meaning within the earthly story; whereas others wouldn't 'hear' anything more than a story which they couldn't object to or make trouble about.

    Another reason for speaking in parables may be that truths are deeper and more multilayered than facts and so are often best conveyed not by statements, which can distort or over-simplify, but by parables, stories, even poetry. Think of the many messages from God in Scripture that are conveyed in these ways. Apart from all the amazing parables Jesus told, there are the Psalms and the Song of Songs.

    Think also of the truths we can learn from our own and other people's life stories. How about keeping a journal of the ways and means by which God touches your life in the coming weeks?

God, please keep me alert and open to messages from you through anyone and anything, anytime, anywhere.

JEAN WATSON

Galatians

Fiona Barnard writes:

'I feel so terrible. I can never be good enough. I feel guilty all the time.' She puts her face in her hands as if to hide the shame and despair she is experiencing. We have a long conversation. A labyrinth of issues lies behind her outburst. I think to myself: she needs to discover Galatians.

'I struggle with the dogmatism of Christians,' he writes in an email. 'The things I once believed about the Bible, well, I am not so sure any more. They were for when I was young and immature. Isn't the loving thing to be more open-minded?' I admire his honesty, but I wish he would delve into Galatians.

She corners me at a party: 'The church has lost the plot. It's sold its soul to the devil in the interests of being "relevant" and trendy. We need to get back to the commandments. It's all there in black and white.' I splutter over the puff pastry and wonder, 'When did you last read Galatians?'

At work, my friendly manager tells me why she is an atheist: 'There is no proof that God exists and the Bible is true. It is bonkers to trust the authority of an ancient text and dismiss all the others.' I gulp uncertainly. This is the accepted opinion in our postmodern, pluralistic western culture. How do I respond? I think Galatians will help me.

The letter of Galatians was one of Paul's earliest epistles, written to Gentile Christians in Asia Minor who were having a major crisis of faith. Paul writes with great urgency because he fears everything may be lost. The church is under threat because the gospel is under threat. At its heart, the attack is jeopardising the freedom that is God's gift to his people. It is an assault on the work of Jesus on the cross. It is a denial of the liberating power of God's grace. It is a potential disaster.

While the immediate circumstances that the Galatian church faced are very different from our own, its message is right up to date. Amid dogmatism and intolerance, scepticism and a sense of failure we encounter all around us, we need reminding of the amazing truths of Jesus which can release us and set us free.

SUNDAY 29 OCTOBER **GALATIANS 1:1–5**

Getting personal

From the apostle Paul and from all the Lord's followers with me. I was chosen to be an apostle by Jesus Christ and by God the Father, who raised him from death. No mere human chose or appointed me to this work. To the churches in Galatia. (CEV)

Letters seem somewhat quaint in these days of Skype and texts, but there is something very special about handwritten notes between two people. I remember spending a whole day in the British Museum, peering with fascination through glass cases filled with personal correspondence. Somehow historical figures drew closer, their thoughts tantalisingly captured on paper a few centimetres from my eyes.

Today we embark on perusing a personal letter sent to a church from its founder. Staring through the prism of two millennia, we will note some pressing issues for the writer and recipients as they struggle to make sense of faith in Jesus in their context. I pray that we will be excited by the good news which is for us as well as for them.

What may surprise us as we open this letter is the almost brusque way Paul begins. Normally his letters start with praise and thanksgiving and appreciative comments about the addressees. These were people who had responded to his preaching and become followers of Jesus. He had spent time with them. He taught them and prayed for them. He cared a great deal about them. We can read about their relationship in Acts 13—14.

Yet here his greeting seems almost perfunctory. He skips the happy memories and encouraging remarks he usually makes. Something is not right. So what do we note? The greeting is full of Christ and what he has done: these truths will be central in what follows. Paul is also very intent on underlining his own God-given commission as he addresses them. What he writes is not simply good advice or personal opinion. He has the authority of God. This is important. The Galatians need to sit up and take heed. So must we.

'I pray that God the Father and our Lord Jesus Christ will be kind to you and will bless you with peace!' (v. 3). Breathe in this blessing today, and pass it on to those you meet.

FIONA BARNARD

MONDAY 30 OCTOBER   **GALATIANS 1:6–10**

How could you?

I am shocked that you have so quickly turned from God, who chose you because of his wonderful kindness. You have believed another message, when there is really only one true message. (CEV)

Imagine the scene. It is 1833. A group of former slaves, recently granted their freedom through a long-overdue act of Parliament, go to visit William Wilberforce. He has spent a lifetime campaigning for their emancipation and he is excited to hear how they are getting on in their new life. What they report is devastating: 'We have decided we prefer to be slaves after all,' they tell him. 'Someone told us that freedom is overrated. They have just issued us with a whole load of new instructions, so we are busy trying to obey them. We are not really capable of making our own choices and determining our own way in the world.'

If Paul sounds outraged, it is because he is. He is upset, betrayed, shattered, furious. He cannot believe that the Galatian church he planted has exchanged the gospel of freedom for a sentence of slavery. Any message that is not about grace, the undeserved kindness of God in Jesus, is no message at all. If he sounds intolerant, it is because he knows that truth is not negotiable. You cannot have two 'truths' pulling in opposite directions. Paul's fiery attack on the false preachers who have deceived them comes from his passionate love for Jesus' message of grace and for them.

'Watch out!' If you see your friend about to be hit by a car, you are not going to launch into a philosophical argument about traffic. You will shout and grab her. Her well-being is so important that you will go straight to the point, no beating about the bush. There are times when something is so wrong, so harmful, that a measured, cool reaction just is not good enough. We need great wisdom to know when to take a stand—for the sake of Christ.

What truths would you stake your life on?

FIONA BARNARD

TUESDAY 31 OCTOBER   **GALATIANS 1:11–24**

Who do I think I am?

Even before I was born, God had chosen me. He was kind and had decided to show me his Son, so that I would announce his message to the Gentiles. (CEV)

In the market place of ideas, there are numerous stallholders peddling many 'truths'. Each calls out, 'Listen to me! Let me tell you what I think.' It is easy to feel overwhelmed amid religious competition and the clash of philosophies. Who do we believe? How do we know that the Bible in our hands is God's word?

From the beginning of the Church, it has been vital that the teachings of Jesus were accurately preserved. Jesus' twelve disciples were the closest to him and called 'apostles', sent with Christ's message. Their word had authority because Jesus commissioned them and the Holy Spirit empowered them. As the Church spread, all shades of teaching appeared, so faithfulness to Jesus' message had to be measured by what the apostles were preaching and writing.

Paul had not walked with Jesus, but crucially, he had met him in a dramatic encounter on the road to Damascus. There Jesus called him to be an apostle to the Gentiles. Troublemakers in Galatia maintained that Paul wasn't really an apostle. They claimed he was making it too easy for anyone to become a Christian by asserting that new believers did not need to keep Jewish rules: 'He is just a people-pleaser to get converts'.

So here Paul recounts what happened. 'I was as Jewish as they get,' he writes, 'until I met Jesus. He chose me, and in the desert retreat of Arabia, he personally taught me the truth. Peter and Jesus' brother James and other churches confirmed my calling, but my authority is from God. What I preach is directly from him.' This matters to Paul, not because he is power-hungry but because what is at stake is the good news of Jesus for the Gentiles. And that includes us!

Someone challenges you: 'Why is Jesus and the Bible so important to you?' How do you answer?

FIONA BARNARD

WEDNESDAY 1 NOVEMBER   **GALATIANS 2:1–10**

Dealing with difficulty

They had come to take away the freedom that Christ Jesus had given us, and they were trying to make us their slaves. But we wanted you to have the true message. (CEV)

When I was a student, I remember a group of self-appointed doctrine police who scrutinised the 'soundness' of speakers who came to the Christian Union. Starting with the best of motives, their concern was that preachers we invited were faithful to Bible truths. In time, some became so narrow and judgemental that very few speakers seemed eligible to pass their stringent standards.

Here Paul recounts a traumatic incident when he was accused of major error. He was in uncharted territory, because his missionary call was directed to Gentiles. This was novel and demanded a different approach. Until then, the apostles had been preaching to Jews who knew the Old Testament law and had been circumcised as a sign of their commitment to God. Indeed, circumcision had always been the way of entering into the people of God.

When Gentiles became Christians, many Jewish believers assumed they would join the community of faith in the same manner. 'No, no, no,' shouted Paul, 'you are adding a requirement that is not part of the gospel of grace. It is saying Christ's cross is not enough.' Not only was he upset on behalf of recent converts; he was troubled by the allegations against him. Most importantly, he was alarmed by the attack on the gospel of grace. In Jerusalem, he sought the leaders' blessing for the sake of unity.

It is tempting to assume that Christians who think differently from us are wrong. New ventures in evangelism and social action can be targets of suspicion because they are edgy and risky. Here the intrepid Paul demonstrates independence, resisting those who would enslave new Gentile believers, but also endorsing the authority of respected leaders. He is a timely model for dealing with differences.

Pray for a person or a project seeking to be faithful to the truth amid unprecedented challenge and risk.

FIONA BARNARD

THURSDAY 2 NOVEMBER   **GALATIANS 2:11–21**

Feet of clay

God accepts only those who have faith in Jesus Christ. No one can please God by simply obeying the Law... I have died, but Christ lives in me. And I now live by faith in the Son of God, who loved me and gave his life for me. (CEV)

'We trusted him. He was a great preacher, a giant in the church, and he let us down. We cannot believe it!' When misjudgements or moral failures of Christian leaders are exposed, there is huge damage and hurt. We see it all the time, in newspapers and church meetings. When will we learn that even saintly looking types have feet of clay like the rest of us?

Because the truth of the gospel is at stake, Paul does not mince his words. Despite recognising the God-given validity of Paul's message, Peter and Barnabas had gone back on a fundamental tenet of the truth. On the one hand they were saying that the cross had broken down barriers between Jews and Gentiles, but then were refusing to share dinner with non-Jews. Paul was furious. This was a battle that he could not ignore. Their hypocrisy and weakness was a betrayal of grace, and it required public opposition. Barnabas had been his mentor and advocate when he was a new believer, so this must have been especially painful for Paul. Even respected pillars of the church can be wrong, wrong, wrong.

This devastating episode brings to the fore the most beautiful expression of the freedom we have in Jesus: 'I now live by faith in the Son of God, who loved me and gave his life for me.' We don't please God by slavish rule-keeping. It is a message for the Galatians, for Peter and Barnabas, for Paul and for us. Take it with you today. Sing it as you drive or peel the potatoes or lie in bed.

Amid the disappointments of personal issues and church life, look to Jesus. Embrace his undeserved kindness. Wave his truth like a flag: 'Jesus is in me. I live by faith in him alone'. Hallelujah!

If you are living in a fog of guilt or disillusionment, how can today's passage encourage you?

FIONA BARNARD

FRIDAY 3 NOVEMBER   **GALATIANS 3:1–14**

No small print

God gives you his Spirit and works miracles in you. But does he do this because you obey the Law of Moses or because you have heard about Christ and have faith in him? (CEV)

'There is no such thing as a free lunch,' they say, 'and there is no gain without pain either.' We are conditioned to spot the scrounger and to suspect any offer which claims to have no strings attached. Consequently grace can seem elusive or outrageous or an inconceivable con.

When Lucy first heard the gospel, she couldn't quite believe it. She had always tried to be good, but then she was told that her 'righteousness was like filthy rags', which annoyed her a little, because it was actually quite hard work. One day, however, the penny dropped and she saw the cross of Jesus in a new light. She was overwhelmed with a sense of her own unworthiness, and then astounded by what Jesus had done for her by bearing her punishment. Tearfully she clasped grace, God's undeserved favour, and nothing was the same again.

Until, that is, some years later. She went to bed feeling guilty. She hadn't read her Bible for a week because she was too busy running the children's holiday club, too exhausted shopping for the old lady next door, too worn out from endless emails from the church building project. The last straw came with a misunderstanding, when she felt accused of not pulling her weight at the outreach lunch club. How dare they? Hadn't she done more than enough for these insistent people? Come to think of it, why did God seem so demanding?

Lucy, Lucy: listen to Paul's words to the Galatian Christians. God has given you his Spirit, and like Abraham of old, accepts you because of your faith. Don't let any rota, any sense of duty, any manipulation by others, rob you of the joy and freedom that comes as a love gift from Jesus.

If you are overwhelmed today by what you feel you need to do for God, stop a minute and acknowledge what he has done for you (then check what he really wants you to do!).

FIONA BARNARD

SATURDAY 4 NOVEMBER **GALATIANS 3:14–25**

L plates

Does the Law disagree with God's promises? No, it doesn't!… The Law was… supposed to teach us until we had faith and were acceptable to God. But once a person has learned to have faith, there is no more need to have the Law as a teacher. (CEV)

I have come late and reluctantly to driving. I am overwhelmed by how much I need to learn, and how terrifying it is to be in charge of a death machine. Daunted, I set out armed with a driving manual and an expensive instructor. The rules are numerous, and I constantly get it wrong. But I am reminded that the costly process is not an end in itself. It is not for bragging about how many laws I can recite; it is so I will be free to travel and take others with me safely. I am promised that in time, muscle memory will relieve me of information overload and catastrophe.

'I don't like the Old Testament with all its regulations,' someone says. 'Today we just need love.' In his passion for the liberating truth of Christ, Paul insists that the Jewish law was part of the covenant plan, demonstrating God's character and our corruption. But vitally, centuries before the law was given, the Jewish patriarch Abram was accepted by God because of his faith. Now, all peoples, including the Galatians and us, are blessed through his example of fidelity and through his perfect descendant: blessed not because we obey rules, but because Jesus has borne the cost of our moral bankruptcy.

Learner drivers in God's ways, the Old Testament people often could not follow his instruction manual. Consequently, the vehicle did not travel freely in close relationship with him. But Christ has put a different car on the road and passed the test at the cross. By his Spirit, he produces a licence with our name on it and implants spiritual 'muscle memory'. Our delight is to travel in his company, thrilled by the freedom of the roads and basking in the security and intimacy of our bond with him.

What is the relevance of the Old Testament in your journey with Jesus today?
FIONA BARNARD

SUNDAY 5 NOVEMBER   **GALATIANS 3:26—4:11**

Knowing who you are

Now that we are his children, God has sent the Spirit of his Son into our hearts. And his Spirit tells us that God is our Father. You are no longer slaves. (CEV)

'I don't know who I am': I heard it again last night, as I watched a TV programme seeking to reunite long-lost families. Each story is very different as it describes heart-breaking decisions and circumstances when parents and children are separated. However, what is fascinating to note is that a sense of personal identity—who we are—is so closely tied with those who gave us life.

'This is who you are,' writes Paul here. 'You are God's children.' Paul is at pains to underline the wonderful gift of freedom given to all believers. God the Father, the Son and the Holy Spirit have moved heaven and earth to expand the family. For years, the law had been like a childminder to Israel, showing them how to live, but now Jewish believers can enjoy the maturity and liberty of an intimate relationship with a loving Father. In a parallel servitude, the Gentile Galatians had been tied up with false gods, but now as Christians they can relish exactly the same status before God as their Jewish brothers and sisters. Why on earth would they want to give up such an astounding privilege and return to a life of restriction and poverty imposed by foreign (Jewish) ethnic restrictions?

Look in the mirror and say, 'I am a dearly loved child of God.' Don't let anyone rob you of your freedom to be who you are in Christ. Behaving like a captive slave will keep your loving heavenly Father at a distance. Comparing yourself with your brothers and sisters misses the point of being part of a family. Breathe in the Father's delight in you. Breathe out your worship to him—and just be who you are.

How can you celebrate and affirm unity and equality amid diversity in the family of Jesus today?

FIONA BARNARD

MONDAY 6 NOVEMBER   **GALATIANS 4:12–31**

Who is your mother: Sarah or Hagar?

Do you know how I feel right now, and will feel until Christ's life becomes visible in your lives? Like a mother in the pain of childbirth… In the days of Hagar and Sarah, the child who came from faithless connivance (Ishmael) harassed the child who came—empowered by the Spirit—from the faithful promise (Isaac). (*The Message*)

'We can't wait for her to be born,' they told me, as mounting baby paraphernalia seemed to take over the whole house. 'We are so excited!' Now I am not a mother, but I suspect that the baby's arrival is the focus of exhilaration rather than the preceding labour. Only after the pains of childbirth will parents be able to gaze on a fresh little face and say, 'She has my nose, but she has your eyes.' Paul longs to see his converts grow into the likeness of Jesus.

Paul has employed all his rational skill to convince the Galatians of the truth against the lies of the Judaisers. Now he appeals in the language of the heart: 'Remember how we first met? How you took care of me when I was so horribly sick? You saw me at my most vulnerable. You cared for me so generously. I was in no state to manipulate or impress you, and yet you accepted my message. Why do you doubt it now? Why have you been persuaded by these spin-doctors who just want to exploit you for their own purposes? I ache for you like a mother in childbirth, longing to see Jesus' life grow in you.'

He continues to speak of mothers as he recalls the Jewish story of Abraham's two sons: one born of a slave through doubt, the other born of a wife in response to faith in God's promise: 'Do you want to be slaves to the Jewish law when you can be children of faith in Jesus?'

As with a child's unhurried development, the life and likeness of Jesus is formed gently in us, through his Spirit, so that we can be children of faith and not of the law.

Lord, help us not to be slaves to doubt, but children of faith, growing in your likeness.

FIONA BARNARD

TUESDAY 7 NOVEMBER **GALATIANS 5:1–12**

Get out of jail free

Christ has set us free! This means we are really free. Now hold on to your freedom and don't ever become slaves of the Law again. (CEV)

'Why on earth would someone want to go back to prison?' We scratch our heads at high criminal reoffending rates. Yet we fail to notice that when it comes to our faith, we often concentrate on the security of measurable disciplines: obey the ten commandments; do your quiet time each day; don't watch dubious TV programmes; follow your faith community's conventions, etc. It is so much less hassle to know the rules and mostly follow them (with a few lapses) than to live freely in loving response to Jesus' grace with all its risk and uncertainty.

Freedom is a scary gift. We are not used to it: we want to do the right thing. As with the Galatian Christians, someone inevitably appears who is keen to tell us what the 'right thing' is. Circumcision and the Jewish ceremonial law may not tempt us, but a list of 'dos' and 'don'ts' might. 'What a relief,' we say. 'I like having something practical to do, and then I know I have done it and can tick it off the list.' Secretly, we can also measure other people's spirituality on this scale. Continue on this path for long and the demands of 'religion' begin to surround us like bars in a cell. 'I am fed up carrying my cross,' we grumble. 'These non-believers are having a much happier time.'

'This is not what it is about,' shouts Paul, pulling out his hair. 'Jesus has carried this cross for you and now you are free.' The gift is a dynamic relationship, rather than a list of rules. When you really understand what Jesus has secured for you, you will want to be with him, to be like him, to follow where he leads. Trying too hard makes us focus on the rules; being free lifts our focus to Jesus, who is 'altogether lovely'.

'Love God and do what you will' (Augustine). Enjoy the wonder and freedom of that today.

FIONA BARNARD

Loving improvisation

My friends, you were chosen to be free. So don't use your freedom as an excuse to do anything you want. Use it as an opportunity to serve each other with love. (CEV)

'Let's play it by ear.' If you are a talented jazz pianist or a sparky comedian, this is an invitation which will get your creative juices going. It is a summons to bring all your training and passion and intuition to the fore. It is a call to fling wide your imagination and muster your resourcefulness. It will take you to places beyond dogged adherence to a script. Exhilarating and terrifying, this spontaneous freedom will demonstrate your artistic calibre.

Rousseau wrote that 'man is born free and everywhere he is in chains'. Men and women both are constrained by their bodies and their bank accounts, by the circumstances of birth and life experience, by needs and physical limitations. Paul, in this letter to the Galatians, recognises that the law was given because we don't know how to be free without harming ourselves and others. It provided parameters in which God's people could reflect his goodness and care—only constraints are not enough. That is why Jesus, the liberator, came.

However, if we think that our salvation is easy, and a licence to do exactly what we want, we haven't really understood what it means to be free in the Spirit of Christ. The risk and appeal of living in the Spirit is that it is all about love. Love is only love when it is freely chosen. Love cannot be forced. Love does not manipulate. Like the musician or actor, ready to improvise, our response to this radically new way of being cannot be sluggish or negligent. It is about opening our hearts to embrace the new song, the new ballad of love that the Spirit of Jesus is composing in us and through us.

Spirit of Jesus: sing your lovely song through me today in all I do and think and say!

FIONA BARNARD

THURSDAY 9 NOVEMBER   **GALATIANS 5:22—6:5**

Mellow fruitfulness

The fruit of the Spirit is love, joy, peace, forbearance, kindness, goodness, faithfulness, gentleness and self-control… Since we live by the Spirit, let us keep in step with the Spirit. (NIV)

The plums in my garden were abundant last autumn. The vibrant reds and greens were almost flamboyant. I swear I heard one call out, 'Look at me: aren't I gorgeous? Taste me: aren't I sweet?' And so I did. Marvelling at the way flowers had been transformed into fruit. Relishing their mouth-watering delights. Puzzling at last year's comparatively meagre crop. Trying to think how the rain and sun and soil might have made a difference. One thing I did not hear last year or the one before was the whisper, 'Oh dear, why is it so difficult to be a plum? I must try harder….' I am no gardener, but in my humble opinion, it is natural for a plum tree to produce plums. Plums do not need to read manuals, or grit their kernels determinedly or scrabble for a purple disguise. They simply grow to become what they are.

'Be who you are in Christ!' pleads Paul to Christian Gentiles being pressurised to become Jews. 'Don't try to be what you are not. Recognise the Spirit's work, forming Christ in you, producing Jesus-like fruit. Embrace him, not mean-spirited legalism.' Rules monitor behaviour and make us judgemental and proud and jealous. They cannot generate kindness or gentleness, faithfulness or joy in us: only God's Spirit can produce this delightful Christ-like fruit.

The 'let go and let God' sentiment can sometimes be an excuse for laziness. This is not about being passive. Paul makes very practical comments on how to nurture the work of the Spirit as he shapes our character. But what a relief to know that as I focus on Jesus, I will begin to be like him: lovely and sweet and good.

Paul illustrates fruitful life in the Spirit as one where there is forgiveness, support for others and a sense of personal responsibility (6:1–5). Is he calling you to attend to one of these especially today?

FIONA BARNARD

FRIDAY 10 NOVEMBER   **GALATIANS 6:6–10**

Spiritual banking

You will harvest what you plant. If you follow your selfish desires, you will harvest destruction, but if you follow the Spirit, you will harvest eternal life… You will be rewarded when the time is right, if you don't give up. We should help people whenever we can… (CEV)

As a teenager I loved the hymn 'Take my life and let it be consecrated, Lord, to thee.' It expressed my devotion to Jesus, and my longing to give him my time and intellect, my hands, feet and heart. The only problem was the verse beginning, 'Take my silver and my gold.' Although I was hardly rich, that was a little too exacting. It worried me that the Lord might actually take me up on it.

It is so much easier to love people in general, rather than a tiresome colleague in particular. It is wonderful to 'serve the Lord', but when that means setting out chairs or washing up, it is less appealing. It is staggering to clasp God's grace, and frolic in the knowledge that we do not need to earn God's favour. But if we struggle to reach out to other undeserving individuals in kindness, we have probably not grasped the meaning of grace. When Paul encourages the Galatians to 'share every good thing you have' (v. 6), they would have understood this to mean financial generosity. The freedom Paul has been celebrating is freedom to receive *and* express bountiful, practical love.

When my purse was lost recently and I rushed to cancel my cards, the bank clerk asked me to list recent transactions to confirm my identity. I could have replied, 'On the deposit side there is limitless love, salvation, forgiveness, Spirit's power, presence of Jesus, privilege of prayer. In grateful response, I have withdrawn some cash for famine relief and Bible translation, the support of the persecuted church and my local congregation. I have withdrawn patience to listen to Mrs B and time to make a meal for the D family. But the account is never overdrawn.' The clerk would have been bemused, but Paul and Jesus would have understood and smiled.

How is your spiritual bank account looking today?

FIONA BARNARD

SATURDAY 11 NOVEMBER   **GALATIANS 6:11–18**

Life and death

I will never boast about anything except the cross of our Lord Jesus Christ. Because of his cross, the world is dead as far as I am concerned… All that matters is that you are a new person… On my own body are scars that prove I belong to Christ. (CEV)

'Sometimes it takes time in a hospice for people to begin to live.' The chaplain movingly described how a driven businesswoman discovered a fascination for birds, and a lowly cleaner became a prize-winning artist. Slavish attachment to ambition and gruelling work had been replaced by new life. In the face of death, there was an invitation to reprioritise. At last there was time to encounter a whole new world, a new self.

These final words of Paul are written in his own shaky hand, because they are so important to him. In the hospice of our mortal life, dying daily to your own selfish urges, you discover a whole new world, a new self. The only boast worth making is not that you have convinced people to follow the rules, he writes, but that they follow Jesus. The only scars worth having are not circumcision scars, but the persecution scars from being faithful to Christ crucified. The only allegiance worth seeking is not to one particular race, but to God's true people.

As you reach the end of this passionate letter, what do you think is God's message to you? How does the cross speak to you in the struggles of past sin, present inadequacy and future's fears? What will help you live freely in the face of rigid dogmatism ('This is the truth, here in black and white') or spiritual bullying ('You have got to do it this way')? How will you respond to thoughtless tolerance ('We all have different opinions; all you need is that loving feeling…') or sullied scepticism ('No ancient book can have anything to tell me today')? I hope you will keep on being reminded of Paul's words as you walk with Jesus. Keep in step with the Spirit!

Can you write in a sentence one thing that has encouraged you through reading Galatians?

FIONA BARNARD

Generations

Chris Leonard writes:

My dad, aged 91, cuddling his first great-grandchild—he, our family's last survivor of his generation and this tiny baby, the first arrival in hers. How special was that! Following more than a decade of sometimes harrowing sicknesses and then deaths of our other three parents, my husband and I felt a real sense of hope and of blessing being passed on. Whatever happens, our photos of the four generations together will be treasured.

Three months later, our second granddaughter was born—and what joy they both have brought! I wonder, will those girl-cousins research their genealogies after we're long gone? I've done some of that myself; it's fascinating to see the patterns—or lack of them—and to find similarities or huge differences between our lives and those of our ancestors.

It started me thinking—how does God feel about generations? Does he have a purpose for each generation? The Old Testament speaks of promises, blessings and curses passing down the generations and Scripture has plenty of genealogies, tales of inheritance, of family histories, generational squabbles and the relationships between parents and children, as well as advice on how to treat young and old.

I see less generational mixing than there used to be though, within churches as well as blood families. People seem to spend most of their time relating in increasingly narrow age-bands, the danger being that we'll lose touch with and respect for other generations. I don't see that in the way Jesus interacted with other generations and I doubt that it's part of God's plan for us. By adopting his attitudes, might we make a counter-cultural difference?

Surely God meant generations to be a force for good. Though their mixing can be positive or negative, the source of much worry or joy, conflict or support, through all of that will be opportunities for us to grow in his grace. The Bible speaks of parents teaching their children about God and supporting their elderly relations, though these days we tend to leave such things to other agencies. But what of those who lack any blood relations, or have been rejected by them? Many such exist in our fractured, war-torn world. Can they find their DNA, their identity, inheritance, nurture and protection within God's family on earth? Big subjects, these—so let's dip our noses into Scripture and see what we find.

SUNDAY 12 NOVEMBER NUMBERS 1:1–19

Genealogies

'Take a census of the whole Israelite community by their clans and families, listing every man by name, one by one... These are... the men who are to assist you: from Reuben, Elizur son of Shedeur; from Simeon, Shelumiel son of Zurishaddai; from Judah, Nahshon son of Amminadab.' (NIV)

I love the television programme *Who Do You Think You Are?* It traces a few of a well-known person's ancestors, often showing lives far harder than any we can imagine, rather than the privileged connections we might expect. Legend says that my family goes back to the twelfth-century's Robin Hood, which sounds most impressive until you consider the snag that he might never have existed! Another branch begins with poor, ordinary folk, Wesley converts—and Christians in every generation since. I thank God for that inheritance and look forward to meeting those ancestors in heaven some day!

Some people spend much time and money tracing their ancestors. God appears interested too, or why would the Bible list so many genealogies? I wonder, though, how many of us have read the lists in Numbers 1 before. What do you see there? Individuals, families, tribes, land, a sense of time—it's all very 'earthed'. God, who is outside space and time, who was and is and is to come and who himself had no forebears, is not in the least airy-fairy or distant when it comes to relating to human beings on this planet. So many people's names, along with the names of their fathers, lands and tribal ancestors, are listed in God's book! And although our own names may not appear in the Bible, Revelation speaks of Jesus' true disciples' names being written in the Lamb's book of life. God's plan was always for one generation after another to worship and follow him: he is concerned for all of our physical and spiritual inheritance.

Thank you, Lord, that you're interested in families, in generations past and yet to come, in individuals and in us!

CHRIS LEONARD

MONDAY 13 NOVEMBER — **PSALM 68:3–10**

Generations in God's family

A father to the fatherless, a defender of widows, is God in his holy dwelling. God sets the lonely in families, he leads out the prisoners with singing. (NIV)

I'm often touched by the bond of deep affection between the very old and the very young. God's plan was that we should all live in supportive families, with different generations loving and helping one another. But in this fallen world children are orphaned and some people reach helpless old age with no living relation left alive to care for them. Family members are separated by marital break-ups, wars, refugee crises, mental illness, addiction, prison—or simply because we're now able to travel, move, live and work far away from our birth-families.

A preacher told how, when he was a young teenager, his parents divorced acrimoniously—and neither wanted to care for him. All too often such rejection passes its damage down the generations. Yet a Christian couple took this lad into their home. They had no blood relationship to him yet parented him wonderfully. He's now a father of two fine sons and works with a Christian charity, helping refugees in conflict zones. What an example of the verses quoted above—of how, working through his people, God can reverse the effects of human fallenness.

So… could you mother someone who is mother- or grandmother-less, or whose mother is incapable of showing love? Do you know a lonely person who might enjoy being included in your family somehow—perhaps as an honorary granny or aunt? When our children were small, various single church friends sometimes came on holiday with us. We had such fun and we all benefited a great deal.

Lord, help us to do what we see you doing—embracing and including the lonely, widowed, orphaned, refugee, even discharged prisoners. Open our eyes to see who needs our tangible, practical love and inclusion in our family.

CHRIS LEONARD

TUESDAY 14 NOVEMBER   **JOHN 1:11–14**

Jesus' generations

He came to that which was his own, but his own did not receive him. Yet to all who did receive him, to those who believed in his name, he gave the right to become children of God—children born not of natural descent, nor of human decision or a husband's will, but born of God. (NIV)

When he was a very small boy, my uncle had to stay at home from Sunday school because of a cold, but jumped with joy when the rest of the family returned. 'Mummy, Mummy, I've learnt all the begattings from Adam to Jesus!' Prodigiously intelligent, he went on to become Dean of an Oxford college, though sadly not to develop a faith.

So, what's the point of Jesus' genealogies in Matthew 1:1–17 and Luke 3:23–37? Oddly, both trace Jesus' ancestors through Joseph, not Mary, who was his only biological relation, and each differs as to the name of Joseph's father. On the grounds that 1 Timothy 1:4 and Titus 3:9 say we're not to become obsessed by 'endless' or 'foolish' genealogies, I'm not going to attempt to untangle all of that here, yet there are things we can learn.

Jesus' genealogies feature surprising people: women, including a prostitute, and foreigners; flawed heroes of faith like Abraham and David alongside Enoch who 'walked with God' flawlessly; some seriously evil kings alongside many individuals we never hear of elsewhere—Abihud anyone? Luke ends with: 'the son of Adam, the son of God', a phrase that applies both to us and to Jesus, with the difference being that our 'blood line' became tainted before his death and resurrection restored it, while Jesus' sonship remained strong and unsullied throughout. It struck me that Luke's genealogy follows Jesus' baptism, when a voice from heaven proclaims: 'You are my Son… with you I am well pleased.'

Blood families can be great… or disastrous. Far better is our adoption into God's family, where generations stretch back to the dawn of time and where we all have an honoured place.

Thank you, Lord, for giving us the right to become your children—not from natural descent, nor because of our parents' decision, but born again of you. May each hear you say, 'My beloved daughter, I'm pleased with you!'

CHRIS LEONARD

WEDNESDAY 15 NOVEMBER   **LUKE 18:15–30**

Entering like children

'Let the little children come to me, and do not hinder them, for the kingdom of God belongs to such as these. Truly I tell you, anyone who will not receive the kingdom of God like a little child will never enter it.' (NIV)

What aspect of children did Jesus mean—their innocence? There's plenty of evidence for original sin, without resorting to Adam and Eve's. All children are born self-centred: they have to learn sacrificial, *agape* love.

'Why don't we hold a pillow over his face?' I asked my mum. At least that's the story I've been told. I remember nothing of this, being three at the time. Of course, Mum didn't follow my remedy for the screaming demands of my baby brother and I've never committed murder, nor gone on to harm my brother—indeed, we had a great holiday together with my father recently. Yet although three-year-old me didn't understand the terrible implications of my words, they were self-centred. My baby brother's needs were depriving me of attention that had been mine.

If it's not about innocence, what aspect of little children must we resemble to enter God's kingdom? Perhaps there's a clue in the second part of our reading. The rich young ruler had everything—power, wealth, status: the children and their mothers had little or none of those. Adult men had pre-eminence in their culture and religion but it was the needy who Jesus reached out to and blessed—the no-hope thief on the cross who became perhaps the very first to be with him in paradise, the sick who were healed. When the Twelve disputed which of them was greatest, Jesus said only the last and the least, as he welcomed a child to illustrate his point (Mark 9:33–37).

To enter God's upside-down kingdom we need to know that we need him. But once we're there, once we know him—we're still needy, of course, but do we then grow in him, bearing the fruit of the Spirit and spiritual children of our own?

Lord, help us to be like children, who arrive with overwhelming needs, then begin to grow up and learn to love others. Yet keep us dependent on you in an independent age, and with a child's wonder in a cynical one.

CHRIS LEONARD

THURSDAY 16 NOVEMBER   **MATTHEW 21:12–17**

Learning from children

When the chief priests and the teachers of the law saw… children shouting in the temple courts, 'Hosanna to the Son of David,' they were indignant… Replied Jesus, 'Have you never read, "From the lips of children and infants you have ordained praise"?' (NIV)

If only those religious leaders had learnt from the children, who understood Jesus so much better than they did, that first Palm Sunday! 'Hosanna' doesn't mean 'praise God', as I thought it did for a long time. It means 'Please save us!' and Jesus' quotation from Psalm 8:2 continues 'against your enemies, to silence the foe and the avenger'. God doesn't work through the mighty and strong but through those who know that they are weak and needing his help. Older generations can learn that from children.

The many young families in my former church were so excited because our excellent drama group was putting on a production of *Paddington Bear*, just for them. We booked our tickets but, the day before that first performance, our small daughter started running a high temperature. Our son saw her all hot and listless in the morning, so we explained that he'd go with Daddy while I stayed at home to look after her. 'No,' he insisted, 'she will miss Paddington. We'll pray to Jesus and he will make her better.' Being considerably more solicitous towards his younger sibling than I had been to mine, he ran over to her and prayed himself, out loud. Later he was most upset when she was still too poorly to go.

That night, however, she slept well and by the next day had become her normal healthy self again. We had no tickets for that second and final performance but her best friend's family kindly took her with them. Jesus had heard our small son's trusting and unselfish cry for help and we parents learnt something about faith, hope and love that day from him.

Lord, at times I've seen children more as a noisy nuisance than as people I can learn from; yet you saw the money-changers and religious leaders as the noisy nuisances and the children as truth-bearers. Help me!

CHRIS LEONARD

FRIDAY 17 NOVEMBER   **LEVITICUS 19:3, 32**

Older generations

Stand up in the presence of the aged, show respect for the elderly and revere your God. I am the Lord your God. (NIV)

A joke goes something like: 'When I was six I thought my parents knew everything. When I was 16 I could see they knew absolutely nothing. Now I'm 26 and amazed at how much they've learnt in ten years!'

If our parents are still alive when we're 76, the relationship is likely to be on a very different basis—and it's not unusual to live to 100+ these days! While parents once looked after us, we may well end up caring for them whilst struggling with our own health or mobility issues. Respecting our parents, honouring them—it's not a given, is it? Not in real life. I guess that's why God put it right there in the ten commandments: 'Honour your father and your mother, so that you may live long in the land the Lord your God is giving you' (Exodus 20:12). Relating to older generations, especially parents, can be fraught—and relationships are everything to God. If I consider the way Jesus the Son related to his Father in heaven, I realise how very far I am from following his example.

I grew up in a loving Christian home yet was still stroppy and critical of my parents during my teenage years. But what if your parents are bad? I remember one lovely Christian guy at university speaking of his struggles to honour a dishonest dad who was often drunk and would swear, hit out and seemed to care nothing for his family or anyone else. 'I can't respect most of the things Dad does, but I do try to honour him through service—like mowing the grass—and I pray God's blessing on him.' What a mature and godly attitude! The Lord doesn't simply issue commands: he offers us his strength, his love and his way to live.

Lord, help me to respect, honour and encourage those who are older than I am, as I respect and honour you, because there's a spark of you in everyone: old or young, good or bad.

                                                                        CHRIS LEONARD

SATURDAY 18 NOVEMBER   **JOEL 2:25–32**

Learning from the old

I will pour out my Spirit on all people. Your sons and daughters will prophesy, your old men will dream dreams, your young men will see visions… both men and women. (NIV)

The society in which many of us live seems to have a cult of the young, whereas in biblical times people respected the wisdom of the old, of wise elders, as they do in much of the developing world today. After university I joined a church consisting mainly of people in their 20s—and a growing number of small children. We had prophecies, visions and many good things happened but, looking back, I sense we missed out on the wisdom of older generations. Joel's prophecy, repeated in Acts 2, suggests that God has plans for every generation.

For the past 20 years I've been part of a church with a good age range. The older people seemed quiet and at first I didn't take much notice of them—they didn't spout head-knowledge and, except when the whole church waited on God over a specific issue, rarely prophesied or shared visions. Failing to look for the wisdom that springs from a lifetime of walking with him, I assumed they'd be inflexible, like in that other joke: 'Mr Jones, you've been a member of this church for over 50 years—you must have seen a lot of changes?' 'Yes, and I've opposed every single one of them!'

But the older people in my church turned out to be pure gold. Unassuming, yet sure of their faith and that God loved them, they could be as flexible to his will as any youngster. They listened to him, weren't judgemental, walked humbly and loved mercy. Great at service, caring, practical love, encouragement, prayer, gratitude, patience—not all of them, all of the time, of course. But how special to have 'parents'—and 'grandparents'—in the faith close by, in these days when blood families are often scattered around the world.

Is the Lord encouraging you to get to know some older people better? Or, if your hair is turning silver (at the roots, anyway) could you be a wise granny to some of the younger women?

                                                                      CHRIS LEONARD

SUNDAY 19 NOVEMBER   **EXODUS 12:17–28**

Teaching the young

'When you enter the land... observe this ceremony. And when your children ask you, "What does this ceremony mean to you?" then tell them, "It is the Passover sacrifice to the Lord, who passed over the houses of the Israelites in Egypt and spared our homes."' (NIV)

Teaching the young about spiritual things is a challenge, a responsibility and also a privilege for parents, aunts, children's workers—the whole church family. I guess the best way to do it is by example—being just, loving, forgiving, showing humility, kindness, patience, providing safe boundaries... We can pray with children, read the Bible and worship with them. We can make it clear that Jesus is at the centre of our homes and lives.

   Mind you, there was a time when that last one misfired for us. We'd been away on holiday. On arriving home we unstrapped our young son from the car. He raced to the front door and kept ringing the bell while we were still retrieving his sister and all her baby-goods. 'Please stop making all that noise!' I called. 'We'll be there in a minute and anyway, you know no one's inside to answer your ringing.' He was most indignant. 'But you said Jesus lives in our house!' Get out of that one with a three-year-old!

   I'm intrigued by the way Jewish festivals—and monuments—were set up partly to teach children, to pass the knowledge of God down the generations by provoking young ones to ask questions. Another example comes from Joshua 4:6–7: 'In the future, when your children ask you, "What do these stones mean?" tell them that the flow of the Jordan was cut off before the ark of the covenant of the Lord. When it crossed the Jordan, the waters of the Jordan were cut off. These stones are to be a memorial to the people of Israel for ever.' Can you dream up similar kinds of learning opportunities for the youngsters you know?

Lord, help us teach the upcoming generation about you. Show us how best to do it with each child we know. And keep us praying for them, because only you can save!

CHRIS LEONARD

MONDAY 20 NOVEMBER **LUKE 2:28–35**

Middle generation

Simeon… said to Mary, [Jesus'] mother: 'This child is destined to cause the falling and rising of many in Israel, and to be a sign that will be spoken against, so that the thoughts of many hearts will be revealed. And a sword will pierce your own soul too.' (NIV)

'The sandwich-generation' or 'piggies in the middle'—it's tough when stroppy teens fight you on one front, while on the other the problems of increasingly needy parents seem to have no workable solutions. The middle-aged group, who often run churches, also often struggle with keeping both youngsters and older people happy, safe and on track.

I haven't found a close parallel with this in scripture but Mary and Joseph are clearly caught 'in the middle' in a way that's beyond what we can know. Charged with bringing up a child who is also God and destined to save, bring peace and light but also discord and sorrow—there's no rule book for that. They must have struggled and made some mistakes, yet they did it! Then I thought of the extreme example of parental agony as Mary saw Jesus nailed on the cross between two criminals, suffering an unimaginable death, the agonies of both flesh and spirit. Jesus is dying for love yet at the same time he knows how his death must hurt his mother, friends and Father.

We can draw strength and hope from all these events. We see two parents doing the impossible, which becomes possible when, having accepted the task God has charged them with, he gives them his help.

And we see that Jesus understands all the tensions, the conflicting 'pulls', the sleepless nights, even the agony of knowing that doing the loving and even self-sacrificial thing may sometimes hurt someone you love.

Looking back on my own life I can remember two occasions when my husband and I were 'in the middle' of seemingly impossible generational problems and Jesus wrought a miracle for us. That should teach us to trust him when the next problem arises!

Lord, help us to ask for your help and then to trust you when problems arise between the generations in our family.

CHRIS LEONARD

TUESDAY 21 NOVEMBER   **2 SAMUEL 18:31—19:7**

Dealing with different generations

The king was shaken. He went up to the room over the gateway and wept. As he went he said: 'O my son Absalom! My son, my son Absalom. If only I had died instead of you—O Absalom my son, my son!' (NIV)

Rape and incest by one son provokes his fratricide by another—then it gets worse! This isn't some lurid drama from the television, but the Bible's extraordinarily honest account of the family of the best king Israel ever had. David might have had a close relationship with God, as revealed in his psalms, and even behaved in an exemplary fashion towards his elders before he became king but, my goodness, his parenting skills were questionable—and had dire consequences.

2 Samuel tells how David fails to resolve issues raised by his son Absalom's killing of another of his sons, Abner, in revenge for Abner's incestuous rape of his half- and Absalom's full sister, Tamar. Absalom stages an initially successful coup against his father's throne, and when David flees Jerusalem, humiliates his father by having sex publicly with David's concubines as well as trying to kill him. In the ensuing battle, Absalom is caught by his hair in an oak tree, then killed by having three javelins thrust in his heart, whereupon David's utter devastation at the loss of his treacherous son risks alienating his own supporters.

Later things improve a little but the seeds of Israel splitting from Judah (the root of all the Samaritan trouble, religious and political rebellion and great suffering) were sown by David and his descendants. Somewhere along the line, power corrupts—dynastic power more than most, perhaps. The behaviour of the kings that follow make far from edifying reading!

I hope whatever happens in your family is never as bad as what happened in David's. Yet you might want to read the whole story, considering prayerfully what you can learn—about pain, perhaps, and about consequences, or the importance of right relationships between generations.

Read the story prayerfully, from 2 Samuel 13 onwards.

CHRIS LEONARD

WEDNESDAY 22 NOVEMBER   **LUKE 13:31–35**

When it all goes wrong

'Jerusalem, Jerusalem, you who kill the prophets and stone those sent to you, how often I have longed to gather your children together, as a hen gathers her chicks under her wings, and you were not willing. Look, your house is left to you desolate.' (NIV)

I am always losing things—my keys, that important piece of paper I know I put down on the desk two minutes ago—it wastes time and infuriates me. But the real agony came when, for a while during our son's difficult teenage years, it seemed as if we were losing him.

In chapter 15 of his Gospel, Luke records Jesus' stories about a lost sheep, coin and son. None of those is really about losing things but about the joy in heaven when a person who is lost turns around—that is repents—and is found again.

The most powerful of those three 'lost' stories concerns the lost son. We see God's extraordinary father-heart as the father runs to meet his prodigal son, just as we see Jesus' desire to gather the lost people of Jerusalem as a mother hen gathers her chicks under her wings. In Luke 19:41 we see Jesus' tears when they refuse to come to him, losing their chance of shalom peace, wholeness, well-being in right relationship with God. The three persons of the Godhead, who love Jerusalem and its people, know the pain of it all going wrong.

We thank God that our relationship with our own son, which went so wrong for a while, is now a happy one. But just as Jerusalem didn't turn to Jesus en masse, so generational divisions within and outside families aren't always healed. As we keep praying, hoping, and loving as far as is possible, it's good to know that God understands and himself does everything he can to heal such relationships and bring restoration and new life.

Lord, you have the heart of a mother as well as a father. Even in heaven, Jesus, you intercede for us. We pray now for fractured families and for all who have turned from you.

CHRIS LEONARD

THURSDAY 23 NOVEMBER JOHN 9:1–7, 24–41

Generational curses and blessings

'You were steeped in sin at birth; how dare you lecture us!' And [the Pharisees] threw him out. (NIV)

When reading this story, bear in mind that Jesus' people were steeped in words from the law such as Numbers 14:18 which says: 'The Lord is slow to anger, abounding in love and forgiving sin and rebellion. Yet he does not leave the guilty unpunished; he punishes the children for the sin of the parents to the third and fourth generation.'

And indeed we can still see patterns of harmful behaviour passing down family lines. These days it tends to be covered by the term 'disadvantaged background'. Yet the best of parents may make harmful mistakes, while those damaged by bad parents may become good and loving. In the story, not only was the blind man healed, he came to see spiritual truth too. Regardless of whether he or his parents were 'good' or 'bad', Jesus saved him.

Following Jesus' death and resurrection all kinds of people may enter his kingdom as God's adopted sons and daughters, breaking any curses passed down through previous generations or through their own sin. Our parents may once have messed up our lives; as parents we may have messed up our children's—but the great news is that the past of God's children doesn't have to be their future.

Remember, too, the words of the last Jewish prophet before Jesus. The angel quoted Malachi 4:5–6 to Zechariah, applying the words to his yet unborn son, John the Baptist: 'I will send you the prophet Elijah… He will turn the hearts of the parents to their children, and the hearts of the children to their parents' (Luke 1:17). There has always been strife between generations but it's in God's heart to set that right—to bless rather than to curse the relationship between parents and their children, between the older and younger generations.

Lord, thank you for breaking the curse brought by our sin. Thank you for the miracles of change and life-healing that you still work today.

CHRIS LEONARD

FRIDAY 24 NOVEMBER   **1 TIMOTHY 4:6–15**

Mentoring the next generation

Set an example for the believers in speech, in conduct, in love, in faith and in purity… devote yourself to the public reading of Scripture, to preaching and to teaching. Do not neglect your gift. (NIV)

It's a word we hear a lot, 'mentoring'—but I'm not sure that words always turn into effective action within churches. Perhaps we need to be asking ourselves how we are training up the next generation for leadership, pastoral work, evangelism and all the other things that are needed. How far are we really discipling the next generation, practically? That's what Paul was doing with young Timothy—discipling and mentoring him, by letter and in person. And Jesus called us in the great commission to make disciples, not just converts.

'Youth land' is a country alien to me. Even when young myself I didn't understand or feel at home there, so I'm in awe of youth leaders who draw alongside the next generation and provide effective discipleship and godly mentoring. With the additional pressures young people face today, such as ready access to pornography, peer pressure to become sexually active at an ever younger age, and expanding dangers from the internet and social media, they certainly need all the support they can get.

The realm of writing is one where I've been mentored—and in turn provided mentoring—though, of course, mentoring stretches way beyond writing into life issues. I'm so grateful to the individuals who've helped, supported and guided me—and now I love helping others in a similar way. Not all are younger than I am in years, only in writing experience. You might be mentoring and discipling a 'baby' Christian far older than you are. For eleven years I led a church home group with a good age-range where we all learnt from one another. Have a think about who is mentoring you—and who you're discipling. In what areas are you called to be doing those things?

Lord, thank you that you don't ask us to walk this walk of faith alone. Show us who you want to guide us—and who we might guide ourselves.

CHRIS LEONARD

SATURDAY 25 NOVEMBER   **1 CORINTHIANS 13:9–13**

The perfect generation?

When I was a child, I talked like a child, I thought like a child, I reasoned like a child. When I became a man, I put the ways of childhood behind me. For now we see only a reflection as in a mirror; then we shall see face to face. (NIV)

'Si jeunesse savait; si vieillesse pouvait' goes the French proverb. 'If only youth knew, if only age could'—what might be achieved in this world? When a child I longed to be older and able to do more things. Now I'm sliding from the middle into the final third of life I look enviously at the young, yet also worry for them.

Looking back, I'm not convinced that all the triumphalist songs my church sang about what our youthful generation would achieve in Christ were true or helpful. Did we fail? What were we meant to achieve? Can any generation follow Christ perfectly? As our Bible readings have shown, generations need each other—despite, or perhaps because of, the frictions between us. Maybe it is they that teach us unconditional love, the kind of love Jesus showed and the kind Paul writes of in 1 Corinthians 13. Surely that's what we're meant to 'achieve' in this life. It may not be considered an achievement by many because it's an attitude, a way of seeing and a way of being. One sign of maturing in Christ will be that we live out that love more and more.

People from every generation can have and grow in faith, hope and love. But what we see of those qualities now, and even what we see of the Father, Son and Holy Spirit, are but faint, imperfect images of the unimaginable glory and beauty that is to come.

When all generations come together, face to face with God, we will know in fullness and be fully known. But maybe we're being 'expanded' now, so that we can increase our capacity to experience that light and love in all its fullness, as we stand as one people before the throne of God. Let's pray Paul's prayer below.

'May the Lord make [our] love increase and overflow for each other and for everyone else… [and] strengthen [our] hearts so that [we] will be blameless and holy in the presence of our God and Father' (1 Thessalonians 3:12–13).

CHRIS LEONARD

There's no place like home

Liz Pacey writes:

I have just returned from taking our dog Jojo for a walk along the tenfoot. If you have no connection with the 2017 City of Culture, Hull, you probably won't know what I am talking about. Tenfoot is our word for back alley. It doesn't sound very glamorous, does it? But for me it is an important part of home! A place where I can let my dog play ball and burn off some of that energy that has my husband Norman threatening to eat his food. A place where I might meet the neighbours and exchange a friendly greeting. I don't necessarily know all their dogs' names, but Diesel, Maggie, Levi and Mollie always have a bark for me. A place where greenery strays out of gardens and turns city into country. A place where I can pray. And think. And sing. And even dance a little, till I remember I could be watched… I have lived here 25 years now, the longest ever in one house. And I love my home. Yes, sometimes I get itchy feet, and sometimes it is nice to go away, but… there is no place like home.

I love the film *The Wizard of Oz*. It is a real feel-good film, the kind you want to watch on a rainy day, surrounded by home comforts. The words that most stick in my mind are the ones that bring Dorothy and her wonderful red shoes home from her magical adventures. Three clicks of the heels and the words 'there's no place like home' and she is back in her own bed. But she isn't the same girl. We see her 'dream' characters have their counterpart in real life, and time away from home has brought new perspectives.

Sadly not everyone has happy memories or feels good thoughts about home: there are the homeless; those for whom home may be a prison; those who are never able to settle long enough in one place to put down roots; or tragically have their roots pulled up.

This week we will be challenged to understand more of the different roles home can play in people's lives and perhaps gain new perspectives on our own view of home.

SUNDAY 26 NOVEMBER   **LUKE 9:57–62**

A place to go from

Still another said, 'I will follow you, Lord; but first let me go back and say goodbye to my family.' Jesus replied, 'No one who puts a hand to the plough and looks back is fit for service in the kingdom of God.' (NIV)

Dundee seemed a very long way from Middlesbrough when I set out to university for the first time. Mam, going home from the railway station to an empty house, resisted the temptation to jump on the train with me. Many years later she told me how hard it had been to let her only child go out into the unknown. But she recognised that the time had come for me to fly the nest. My first sight of Dundee was across a long rail bridge over the wonderful River Tay. I felt a heady mix of apprehension and excitement. My new life had begun. For two of my student years I had rooms that overlooked that beautiful view. And depending on my mood it spelled out either more adventures… or just occasionally a longing for the security of home. Today's Bible reading is a really exciting passage about going out into the unknown. Jesus makes no bones of the fact that if we want to follow him the only way is forward.

One man wants to say goodbye to his family, one man wants to bury his father. We might think these were both valid reasons for delaying. And would Jesus *really* be unsympathetic in these situations? But sometimes we can convince ourselves we are needed at home when it is really an excuse not to take that next step into the life we are called to. It is easy enough saying we will follow Jesus anywhere but not always so easy to do. And sometimes serving Jesus at home can be the hardest option, waiting and watching while others seem to have all the excitement. Wherever we are, Jesus calls us to follow him.

If we are the ones left at home what positive things can we do? Pray for young people as they start to make their own way in life.

LIZ PACEY

MONDAY 27 NOVEMBER — LUKE 15:11–31

A place to go back to

'So he got up and went to his father. But while he was still a long way off, his father saw him and was filled with compassion for him; he ran to his son, threw his arms round him and kissed him.' (NIV)

Nine years or so after my first big adventure I was home, with my tail between my legs. Well… not quite. In my twenties I suffered from depression and agoraphobia and Mam made the circuitous train journey from Middlesbrough to Cambridge to rescue me and bring me home. She nurtured and supported me through the next troublesome months. If she didn't quite hold my hand when I went out she put a dog lead in it (with dog attached!) which had much the same positive effect. I had retained my close relationship with my mother through my years away so was able to send out a cry for help. Her response was immediate.

The prodigal son had a much harder time, brought on entirely by himself. He couldn't wait to get away from his loving father. His father didn't stop him leaving, but I'm guessing never a day went by when he wasn't thinking of him. And as time passed the boy came to see what he had lost. The father may not have been able physically to go out and rescue him but he was at home waiting and watching, hoping against hope for his return. The son had learnt a lot about life while he had been away and he knew he had to apologise to his father for the way he had behaved. He probably suspected there would be trouble from his brother. He didn't expect to stroll back in as if nothing had happened. He certainly didn't expect the wonderful love and welcome he received from his father. Unconditional love. What a wonderful picture of God's love for us.

'For I know the plans I have for you,' declares the Lord, 'plans to prosper you and not to harm you, plans to give you hope and a future' (Jeremiah 29:11).

LIZ PACEY

TUESDAY 28 NOVEMBER — NEHEMIAH 2:1–18

A place to work on

I was very much afraid, but I said to the king, 'May the king live forever! Why should my face not look sad when the city where my ancestors are buried lies in ruins, and its gates have been destroyed by fire?' (NIV)

I went into the city centre one day last year, and found myself confused and overwhelmed. There were orange barriers here, cones and signs of 'road closed' there. Everywhere ramps spanned the way over huge holes in the ground to allow entry to shops. I was in Hull during the 2017 City of Culture preparations. A lot of work was going in to make our city even more attractive and user-friendly than it already was. There was great jubilation when we heard we had been chosen (especially among the Knitwits—a group of knitting enthusiasts—as we featured albeit briefly in the promotional video!) and it wasn't long before the community started coming together and getting into the swing of things.

The cause of chaos and devastation in Jerusalem was much more serious. Nehemiah has prospered away from his home and is now working in a royal household. But he has not forgotten his roots and when his brother visits bringing news of the distress of their people, he immediately feels their pain. They have survived exile and now are fighting to restore their broken home city. Nehemiah yearns to help. He might have thought there wasn't much he could do from a distance. But he knows he can seek God's help. So, after much prayer he approaches the king, and in fear and trembling tells him the situation. And the king grants him the time to go and do what he needs to do. He has the practical skills, he puts in the preparation. Above all he has the ability to get his community working together towards a common good. We can learn a lot from him!

We might not have such a huge impact on our home town as Nehemiah did. But there are things we can do. Ask God to show you where you can make a difference in your community.

LIZ PACEY

WEDNESDAY 29 NOVEMBER   **GENESIS 18:1–10**

A place of welcome

He said, 'If I have found favour in your eyes, my lord, do not pass your servant by. Let a little water be brought, and then you may all wash your feet and rest under this tree.' (NIV)

My friend stretched out on our settee and said: 'I feel very peaceful here.' What higher compliment about my home could I ask for? Over the years we have had many friends and relatives staying with us in our little house. It has been a bit of a tight fit sometimes but I do hope we have made everyone feel welcome. I love having people to stay. I might panic a bit as I prepare. Now… where did I leave the coffee table… oh yes, it's under that pile of books and knitting… But I get there in the end, even if my husband can't understand what all the fuss is about.

In our reading today an act of hospitality covered by a few words must have taken an age of preparation. I have to confess that Abraham's preparations for his guests were rather more lavish than mine ever are. I do wonder if his wife and the servants were quite so chuffed that they had to rustle up a feast at such short notice. Perhaps Sarah was inside the tent going frantic about Abraham just taking in these people off the street. But noon was the time when passing strangers might need rest and refreshment in their long journeys and hospitality was a fact of life. Perhaps today we think we are too busy to take time to be hospitable, but sometimes a true welcome is just to let people take us as they find us. A cup of tea and a comfy settee might be all they really need.

'Do not forget to show hospitality to strangers, for by so doing some people have shown hospitality to angels without knowing it' (Hebrews 13:2). Do you ever stop to think you might be entertaining angels?

                                                                              LIZ PACEY

THURSDAY 30 NOVEMBER   **LUKE 2:36–52**

A place in God's house

After the festival was over, while his parents were returning home, the boy Jesus stayed behind in Jerusalem, but they were unaware of it. Thinking he was in their company, they travelled on for a day. Then they began looking for him among their relatives and friends. (NIV)

I think any parent reading the above verse will get a shiver of something like disbelief down their spine. How *could* Mary have been so blasé about her son's whereabouts? She was confident in the care of her extended family. But also, perhaps without even realising it, she had a sense that wherever Jesus was he had his heavenly father's protection and needed to be about his business.

My friend's twelve-year-old grandson came to church with her for the first time recently. Within minutes the welcome team made him feel so comfortable and at home he was joining them handing out hymn books.

Of course, the boy Jesus had very good reasons to feel at home in the temple. He had been there as a baby and had been continuously prayed for by Anna. He had doubtlessly been lovingly told the story of that first visit many times, been schooled in the traditions, and already learned to respect what he knew of the place. Most of all, it was his Father God's house. And he was confident about his place there.

Another friend of mine tells of her experience of God's house as a small child. She couldn't quite understand why he never actually seemed to be there when they went to see him. But she knew he had lots of houses and just thought he must have been at one of the others. Churches can seem very strange places to the young. And to the not-so-young! We have a lot of responsibility to help young people and strangers feel as at home in God's house as we do.

Spend some time thinking, and praying, about how you can be more welcoming to people at church, remembering that sometimes it isn't only new people who need help to feel at home.

LIZ PACEY

FRIDAY 1 DECEMBER LUKE 10:38–42

A place to be myself

As Jesus and his disciples were on their way, he came to a village where a woman named Martha opened her home to him. She had a sister called Mary, who sat at the Lord's feet listening to what he said. (NIV)

It was Lent 2016 and the Archbishop was off on a Pilgrimage of Prayer, Witness and Blessing across the Diocese of York. Walking, talking, preaching, teaching each day he met many people and must have been exhausted each evening when he was welcomed into a parishioner's home for the night. I wonder if he ever wished he could just go home to his own bed. I wonder if any of the hostesses felt pressurised by all the preparations as Martha did, or if they were able to relax and enjoy their guest's company like Mary. Hopefully by the time he arrived the chores were done and they could savour the experience. Not many of us get to have an archbishop come to stay!

Home really is our castle. Some of us find it hard to let the barriers down and allow others to see us in the place that says so much about us. We may need to learn to be more open. But we also have to be careful not to let home only be a place for others. It needs to be a sanctuary for us too. Hospitality is important, but we can't give out if we are worn out. Sometimes we need to pull up the drawbridge and have time for ourselves and our nearest and dearest. And God. Home is the place where we can kick off our shoes and the traces of the outside world and relax. The place we can express ourselves in our own way. The place where even in a mountain of ironing or cleaning and cooking we can feel blessed and at home with Jesus.

Lord, grant me ears to listen to you as Mary did; hands to serve as Martha did; and wisdom to get the balance right so I can truly be the person you made me to be.

LIZ PACEY

SATURDAY 2 DECEMBER   **JOHN 14:1–4**

A place in heaven

'Do not let your hearts be troubled. You believe in God; believe also in me. My Father's house has many rooms; if that were not so, would I have told you that I am going there to prepare a place for you?' (NIV)

Over the years I have had many homes. From a single room in a nurses' home to a shared flat with friends to my very own house. And finally my move to Hull to set up home with my new husband. Preparations for each move were very different, but each time there was excitement, a sense of moving forward.

That isn't necessarily so as we grow older. We might have to downsize. Or even go into residential care. My mother used regularly to tell me to shoot her if there was any likelihood of her being put into a home. Thankfully she never had to put my daughterly duty to that test. But sadly age does bring frailty and some people do need care that cannot be provided for them in their own houses. The often used phrase 'being put in a home' says so much about perceived loss of independence and choice. How sad it is that the word 'home' can now have such negative connotations. Over the years, through family connections, work and church I have visited many people in care homes. And they can be very far from being places of doom and gloom.

I love this Bible passage. Although short, it contains so much hope and encouragement. It tells us that because we believe in Jesus we have no reason to let our hearts be troubled (v. 1). When we think about it, a lot of our troubles can be related to our homes. We worry about elderly parents, children, paying the bills. But with God's help we will get through our earthly problems.

And then… we are going home to Jesus (v. 3). He has already made all the preparations. All we have to bring is ourselves… and our excitement.

Pray for people living in residential and nursing homes and those who have responsibility for their care. Perhaps there is someone you know that you could visit and make feel special.

LIZ PACEY

Isaiah

Lyndall Bywater writes:

I grew up in a Christian family, but really came to faith in my late teens. In those days, 'salvation' was explained to me through logic and reason. I was led through a little book called 'The Four Spiritual Laws', and encouraged to make an intellectual response to a series of statements—statements about my own sin, about who Jesus was and what he did, and about whether I wanted to choose Christianity. It worked: I made those choices and committed my life to follow Jesus; but it never captivated me.

Knowing what I know now about personality and how it shapes our spirituality, I understand that I was never likely to be thrilled to the core by a set of logical propositions. I am intuitive by nature, and I love abstract things more than concrete things. That means, among other things, that I love ideas more than proofs, stories more than reasons, and (ironically given that I'm blind) pictures more than words.

Some time later, I discovered the book of Isaiah, and it turned my world upside down. Suddenly, instead of rules and rationales, there were multi-media scenes in my head: fantastically colourful images of mountains and deserts, camels and processions, tents and cities. Almost none of them bore any resemblance to 20th-century Britain, but they still spoke more to me about this 'salvation' thing which I'd just chosen than any of the tracts or apologetics lectures.

The latter part of the book of Isaiah (chapters 40—66) is a collection of prophecies given to the people of Israel while they were in exile in Babylon. It is a set of snapshots, showing them God and giving them hope for the future, and in those snapshots is the essence of salvation.

The chapters aren't like a photo album, showing one snapshot after another. They're more like an art enthusiast leading us round a gallery, showing us new works, but every so often being unable to resist the temptation of going back to masterpieces we've already seen.

Given that we only have 14 days, we're going to try and find some order in this passionate chaos, taking one particular image each day and exploring what it communicates to us about salvation. My hope and prayer for you is that you will find your own understanding of salvation growing deeper, richer and fuller as you study these snapshots.

SUNDAY 3 DECEMBER   **ISAIAH 40:1–2, 25–31**

Debt cancelled

'Speak tenderly to Jerusalem, and proclaim to her that her hard service has been completed, that her sin has been paid for, that she has received from the Lord's hand double for all her sins.' (NIV)

Being a freelancer, I find my income can be a little variable at times. Usually I have enough money coming in to offset my outgoings, but once or twice a year, I hit a sticky patch, and the maths just doesn't quite add up somehow. It's in those moments that I turn to my husband, and he willingly rescues my bank balance. Believe me, no one is more aware than me of how blessed I am to have that possibility. It is hard to put into words the joy and relief I feel when I know that the money-gap has been bridged. And my husband, in a lovely little nod to Isaiah 40:2, always puts in about twice as much as my account actually needs.

    Throughout human history, religion has involved being in arrears. People's understanding of gods has always centred around the idea that they have power to affect our lives, and that we need to earn their favour. The people of Israel were surrounded by tribes who lived that way; who were never entirely sure if they had done enough to earn the approval of their exacting, demanding deity. That's why the beginning of Isaiah 40 is such an explosion of joy: it's God, the one true God, rewriting all the rules. It's God, all-holy and all-powerful, telling his people that he's cancelled their debt. They're not in arrears anymore; they don't owe him anything, and they never again have to wonder whether they've done enough to earn his approval.

    Have you slipped into that pattern of viewing God as a capricious deity who you're always trying to make it up to? Today, take comfort in the knowledge that you're not in arrears. In Jesus, your debt is cancelled, your account is in credit and you are loved unconditionally.

Spend some time reading and rereading verse 2. Let those words soak in. Ask God to set you free from feeling you have to earn his love and favour.

LYNDALL BYWATER

MONDAY 4 DECEMBER — **ISAIAH 41:8–20**

A change of soil

'I will put in the desert the cedar and the acacia, the myrtle and the olive. I will set junipers in the wasteland, the fir and the cypress together, so that people may see and know, may consider and understand, that the hand of the Lord has done this.' (NIV)

One of the more illogical facets of my personality is my utter indifference towards gardening, contrasted with my absolute love of Radio 4's *Gardeners' Question Time*. Give me the opportunity to dally awhile among the perennials or coax life from a wilting herbaceous border, and I will throw my hands up in horror and head for the kettle; but, once the tea's made, give me the opportunity to spend half an hour or so listening to a bunch of experts discussing said perennials and herbaceous borders, and I am all ears. The best kind of gardening is the imaginary kind, as far as I'm concerned.

You can't be as devoted a fan of *GQT* as I am without knowing that soil composition is everything. You can have the best plants, the perfect weather and the finest plant-feed products on the market, but if the soil is wrong, the plant just won't thrive.

Living as we do in a land where all kinds of trees grow with relative ease, it can be easy to miss the impact this prophecy would have had on the people of Israel. They lived in a desert land; it was hard to grow much of anything, especially trees. Yet God promises a veritable forest!

Salvation isn't just about being forgiven; it's about being repotted: taken from the desert soil of making do on your own, and transferred to the rich soil of life in the company of God himself. In this new soil, all kinds of things can grow—things you never dreamed possible. In this new soil, there is an eternal supply of life and goodness. In this new soil, you don't have to just survive, you can thrive. In this new soil, you can be the person God made you to be.

Are you living as though you're still potted in the old soil? What would it feel like to thrive? What can you do today to help yourself remember that you have been repotted?

LYNDALL BYWATER

TUESDAY 5 DECEMBER   **ISAIAH 40:3–5; 49:11–17**

A change of landscape

'Every valley shall be raised up, every mountain and hill made low; the rough ground shall become level, the rugged places a plain.
And the glory of the Lord will be revealed, and all people will see it together.' (NIV)

Yes, you've guessed it: not only do I love listening to radio programmes about gardening, I also love watching TV programmes about landscaping. In my younger days, when I had more time to watch TV, I used to love wasting an hour or so watching a bunch of imaginative, energetic 'garden professionals' turning the back yard of some mid-terrace home into a good impression of a tropical rainforest. Be reassured though—I am no more tempted to relandscape my own garden than I am to plant anything in it!

We reflected yesterday on the remarkable promise that God has a whole new soil for his beloved people: a soil full of life and goodness. Today, we turn to an even more radical promise, and one which turns up several times in these latter chapters of Isaiah. Today, God isn't just exchanging old soil for new; today, God is reforming the land itself. If transforming soil composition isn't impressive enough, this God of ours can redraw the contours of the landscape with a wave of his hand.

But why would God want to flatten the landscape? Aren't mountains beautiful? Well, of course we're into the realms of metaphor here. God has nothing against mountains—he made them in the first place, after all. These promises are about access, about God wanting his people to know that they can get to him, and he can get to them. This is a loving parent promising that nothing will keep him from the children he loves.

Sometimes the landscape of life can make you feel that God is the other side of an impassable mountain. Today, he wants you to know that he is here, and that nothing can separate you from him. He can flatten that mountain in a moment.

Draw the landscape of your present life: the smooth peaceful places, and the mountainous problems that seem to cut you off from God. As you look at the scene, imagine those mountains being levelled, as your God comes to find you.

LYNDALL BYWATER

WEDNESDAY 6 DECEMBER   **ISAIAH 43:14–21; 48:1–7**

The newest of the new

'This is new, brand-new, something you'd never guess or dream up. When you hear this you won't be able to say, "I knew that all along."'
(*The Message*)

I live in a university city, which means we get two new years every year. There's the January one, with its resolutions and detoxes, and there's the September one, when thousands of new students arrive, and the city smartens itself up for a whole new burst of life and possibility.

Except this year, September rather passed me by. I was feeling depressed. It might say 'new academic year' on the tin, but to me it felt like just another twelve months of the same old same old.

There are two kinds of 'new'. There's renewal, which is what we see in spring, when the land is refreshed by a new sprinkling of all those flowers we love so much but haven't seen for a year, and then there's 'brand-new', which is something completely different. To follow the analogy, brand-new would be like spring bringing in a wave of flowers we've never seen before.

Exile wasn't all bad for the people of Israel. It wasn't slavery, like Egypt, but it was assimilation—being absorbed into the Babylonian way of life. They must have wondered if that was it; if God had given up on them. Perhaps they thought the circle of the year, the rhythm of the seasons in that foreign land, was the only 'new' they would ever see again.

God can always do brand-new. He isn't bound by the laws of the universe or the seasons of our lives. If he wants to grow a whole new species of flower in your garden, he can, and if he wants to write a completely new story in your life, he will, so long as you let him. If you're feeling jaded by the same old same old today, take heart that the God of the Brand-new is on the move.

Are you struggling to believe that the brand-new is possible? Why not buy some seeds or bulbs you've never planted before? Plant them out, and as they grow, let them remind you that life won't always be the same old same old.

LYNDALL BYWATER

THURSDAY 7 DECEMBER   **ISAIAH 54:1–10; 55:1–7**

A call to expand

'Enlarge the place of your tent, stretch your tent curtains wide, do not hold back; lengthen your cords, strengthen your stakes.' (NIV)

What's your preference when it comes to birthday presents? Are you a 'just surprise me with a nice gift' person, or are you more of a 'buy me something I really want or just give me the money' person? I'm definitely the former. In fact I become like a rabbit in the headlights if anyone gives me money. I think it's the pressure of needing to make the most of it. It seems wrong to use it to pay the gas bill, but I can never think of anything special or significant enough to buy with it.

    The Isaiah prophecies depict salvation as more like a voucher than a vase. We often see salvation as something beautiful which has a few handy uses—forgiveness, inner peace, eternal life etc.—but which we don't fully understand, and which, if we're honest, we're a bit afraid to use in case we put a foot wrong and break it. God, on the other hand, describes salvation as a gift to be grabbed hold of; a resource to be made the most of. Like the person who opens the birthday cheque and runs straight to the shops, full of excitement about all the things they can now afford to buy, God wants the life of salvation to be something that expands us; something that challenges us to think bigger than we ever have before.

    The death and resurrection of Jesus didn't just resolve a few awkward issues between us and God, it picked us up out of our limited, shrinking, on-the-way-to-death lives, and set us down in a life which is designed to get bigger, deeper and more and more fulfilling, until we get so full that we outgrow these earthly bodies of ours, and step from this world into something even more beautiful.

Is your faith shrinking or expanding? What can you do to grow a bit more into that glorious salvation gift? Is there something you've always wanted to do but have never had the nerve to try? Why not start on it today?

LYNDALL BYWATER

FRIDAY 8 DECEMBER   **ISAIAH 43:1–13; 44:9–11**

A matchless God

'I, even I, am the Lord, and apart from me there is no saviour. I have revealed and saved and proclaimed—I, and not some foreign god among you. You are my witnesses,' declares the Lord, 'that I am God.' (NIV)

Ancient Babylonia was a land full of gods. There were national gods, regional gods, and even gods of individual households. They had supernatural powers, of course, but they also needed a physical 'body' through which to be present in the world, so someone had to make an idol of them, and that idol needed to be looked after—to be fed, cleaned and clothed. What's more, you didn't dare put a foot wrong. Your idol could bring all kinds of trouble down on your head if you weren't careful.

It was an exhausting business, and it's what God's people were living right in the middle of when they received these prophecies from Isaiah. They were in exile in a land where gods were capricious, petulant, demanding entities. It's no wonder then that God himself came blasting through with these clarion words in Isaiah 43:11. He wanted them to grasp, once and for all, that he is not some unreliable deity who sometimes intervenes and sometimes doesn't; some moody talisman who likes you one day and punishes you the next. He is absolute power, absolute truth and absolute love. He is always at work, he is always right and his affection for us never diminishes.

We know it in our heads, don't we, but how often do our hearts buy into the Babylonian lie that our God is an untrustworthy tyrant who needs appeasing? How often do we doubt his power or try to earn his love? How often do we turn to foreign gods—probably not the Babylonian pantheon of Marduk and co., but perhaps the modern-day pantheon of money, popularity, security and pride?

You don't just have a god. You have the King of kings, the Lord of lords and the God of gods. Now, that's a God worth trusting your life with.

Ancient cultures believed that, for a god to be present in the world, he needed an idol of him, usually in human form. Our God became present in our world in human form—not a man-made statue, but the living man, Jesus Christ.

LYNDALL BYWATER

SATURDAY 9 DECEMBER   ISAIAH 46:1–11; 55:8–13

Carried instead of burdened

'Even to your old age and grey hairs I am he, I am he who will sustain you. I have made you and I will carry you; I will sustain you and I will rescue you.' (NIV)

Have you ever seen a child riding on their dad's shoulders? I remember doing it myself when I was a little girl, and I can still recall the strange, exhilarating contrast of being perched so precariously, so high up, and yet feeling absolutely secure because my dad had hold of my legs, making sure I didn't overbalance and fall off.

If you read through the whole of the book of Isaiah, you'll find a lot of scathing references to idols. You could be forgiven for wondering if God was on something of an ego trip, but since he is absolute in power and glory, we can assume he wasn't having some kind of self-image wobble. The issue is that idols are dangerous and draining for us humans.

Once the Babylonians had washed, fed and clothed their idols, they then had to take them out for walks, parading them through the streets to affirm their greatness. The idols themselves became a burden. To put your trust in anything less than God is life-sapping. When you trust something that is less than God, then you end up being weighed down by it. If it's money, then you have to make enough of it; if it's an addiction, then you need to feed it; if it's another person, then you need to keep pleasing them. Idol-worship is exhausting!

So now do you see the beauty of the contrasting pictures in chapter 46? We can either carry idols, or we can be carried by a God who has arms that are bigger than the universe. We can either slave away, trying to make life good for ourselves, or we can rest on our never-failing God, letting him fulfil his promises and work out his perfect plan for our good. The choice really is ours.

A precious verse in the book of Jonah says: 'Those who cling to worthless idols forfeit the grace that could be theirs' (2:8, NIV 1984). Is there something in your life which is draining you and causing you to miss out on grace?

LYNDALL BYWATER

SUNDAY 10 DECEMBER   **ISAIAH 52:13–15; 53:10–12**

Feeling human again

But many were amazed when they saw him. His face was so disfigured he seemed hardly human, and from his appearance, one would scarcely know he was a man. (NLT)

One of the Catholic Church's newest saints is Mother Teresa of Calcutta. She was famous for many things, but the abiding impression of her is the way she would 'rehumanise' people. She would find those who were in the most destitute circumstances, and she would pick them up, often literally, and care for them. In many cases, poverty and disease had disfigured them terribly, and many people would have struggled to look at them, let alone touch them and tend to their needs, but Mother Teresa had no 'disgust threshold'. She simply got on with it, taking them from the sub-human condition they found themselves in and giving them back their humanity.

When you read the whole of the second part of Isaiah, you start to get the feeling you're in Eden, or in heaven, or both! But Eden and heaven aren't special privileges for the chosen few. They are human life as it was always meant to be. These beautiful promises aren't extra benefits for people in some select God-club; they are pictures of the life we were always meant to live. To be forgiven, to be fruitful, to know that there is always new hope, to be carried by an all-sufficient God; that's human life as God designed it.

The human race threw away that glorious gift of God-forged humanity, and then wondered how to get it back. The solution turned out to be drastic. It could only be done by God himself being willing to inhabit the most dehumanised state imaginable, and there is perhaps nothing the human race has ever devised which is more sub-human than nailing a living person to a cross.

Jesus went there. He became dehumanised, that we might be rehumanised. Through him, we can live the life God always intended us to live.

Jesus Christ, as I joyfully await your birth celebrations, I stop to remember your death. You came that I might have life. When this world disfigures and dehumanises me, help me to put my hope in your all-transforming sacrifice.

LYNDALL BYWATER

MONDAY 11 DECEMBER   **ISAIAH 42:1–9; 61:1–3**

Freedom from captivity

'I, the Lord, have called you in righteousness… to open eyes that are blind, to free captives from prison and to release from the dungeon those who sit in darkness.' (NIV)

When I was a young adult, I spent quite a lot of time doing evangelism: going out on the streets and talking to people about Jesus. We were trained to answer all the tricky questions, and though I was comfortable with most topics that would come up, the one I really hated was that old chestnut about Christianity being just a 'crutch for the weak'. As a strong, confident young woman, I resented the implication that I needed a crutch. As a 43-year-old woman, who regularly doesn't feel either strong or confident, I can now enthusiastically affirm that I have no problem at all admitting that my faith is a crutch for my weakness!

Many people read the latter chapters of Isaiah with a kind of bewildered longing, knowing that these pictures of abundance and blessing are somehow meant for them, but never quite experiencing them as reality. If that's you, then take heart. The reason may be that you're still in prison. Someone in captivity is unlikely to experience the exhilaration of deserts bursting to life, mountains being levelled or tent-curtains being stretched wide. Those things only start to make sense if you know you are truly free.

Whether rich or poor, cared-for or neglected, well-educated or left to our own devices, life tends to build prisons for us. It's the way of a world which has chosen to abandon God and plot its own course. The right question is not 'Am I in prison?' but 'Which prison exactly have I got stuck in?'

The very first line of Jesus' mandate in this world was to set captives free, all of them. That includes you and me. The truth is, we all need a strong deliverer to rescue us and set us free, and his name is Jesus.

Today, ask Jesus to set you free in one particular area of life. When you've done that, why not ask a friend to support you in prayer as you move forward.

LYNDALL BYWATER

TUESDAY 12 DECEMBER ISAIAH 58:1–14; 61:4–11

Paying it forward

'You'll use the old rubble of past lives to build anew, rebuild the foundations from out of your past. You'll be known as those who can fix anything, restore old ruins, rebuild and renovate, make the community liveable again.' (*The Message*)

Jenna spent most of her teenage years living with an eating disorder. She hid it, she fought with it, she gave in to it and she fought it again, and finally she asked for help. After a lot of love, practical care and prayer, she eventually reached a place where it didn't feel that the disorder ran her life anymore. For many years, she avoided anything to do with eating disorders, not wanting to be reminded of what she'd been through, but one day she realised that God was asking her to reach out to other young women who were living the life she'd lived. It was daunting and painful, but she let her own story become a rope of hope for others to grab hold of.

One of the loveliest things about the latter chapters of Isaiah is that it's often nigh-on impossible to work out whether the prophet is talking about Jesus or about God's people. One minute it's Jesus who's the bringer of justice, and the next minute it's us. Of course, the truth is it's both. Jesus springs us from our jails of brokenness, but he intends our freedom to have a domino effect. He's the one who rescues from darkness, but he's partial to partnership, and he co-opts us into his rescue missions wherever he can.

Eugene Peterson's *The Message* paraphrase paints an awe-inspiring picture of us taking the rubble of our past—the very bricks of which our own prisons were made—and using them to build places where others find hope. The recycling process is unlikely to begin immediately—we need time to recover from our wounds and enjoy our freedom—but don't be surprised if, one day, you hear Jesus asking if he can use your past to give someone else a brighter future.

Looking back, is there any 'rubble' from your past which God might be asking permission to use? Can you do something today to give hope to someone who's going through a difficult experience you've been through before?

LYNDALL BYWATER

WEDNESDAY 13 DECEMBER ISAIAH 42:10–25; 60:1–2

Light and darkness

'But I'll take the hand of those who don't know the way, who can't see where they're going. I'll be a personal guide to them, directing them through unknown country. I'll be right there to show them what roads to take, make sure they don't fall into the ditch.' (*The Message*)

As a blind person myself, I can vouch for the fact that blindness can be a complicated business. I went to special school as a child, and was surrounded by children who had varying degrees of sight loss. A very small minority could see nothing at all, but most of us had some residual sight, whether just the ability to detect light and darkness, or enough to read normal text with the use of a magnifier. For our teachers, it was a bit of a minefield. Like all children, we loved to push the boundaries, and we weren't above pretending we could see less than we really could, just to get out of things. Their job was to detect whether we were really that blind, or just faking it.

One of the recurring images in the Isaiah prophecies is the contrast between light and darkness. Salvation is, among so many other things, about being led by the hand out of the darkness of life without God, and brought into the light of his truth and love.

Yet the verses in Isaiah 42 also flag up a different kind of blindness: the kind where we choose not to see. In his paraphrase in *The Message*, Eugene Peterson paints an uncomfortable picture of people who have seen the light, so to speak, but who have stayed shut up in their prisons, licking their wounds. The enemy works hard at making us believe that our own problems leave us no space to look out for other people. Jesus, the Light of the World, has come not only that we might find our own way through life, but also that we might see others in their need and reach out to them. He is the Light of the World, but so are we (Matthew 5:14).

Father God, forgive me when I become so overwhelmed by my own problems that I stop choosing to look outwards towards others. Help me to find perspective, and to open my eyes to see who you want me to see.

LYNDALL BYWATER

THURSDAY 14 DECEMBER   **ISAIAH 49:8–10; 63:1–14**

A shepherd's care

In all their suffering he also suffered, and he personally rescued them. In his love and mercy he redeemed them. He lifted them up and carried them through all the years. (NLT)

Did your parents have aspirations for you when you were young? Did they used to encourage you in a particular career direction? I always remember my mum telling me once that she thought I'd make a great philosopher. At the tender age of 16, I could see her point, but I could also predict that there wouldn't be much of a living in it, so I opted for something more pragmatic.

Had you been born into a fifth-century BC Hebrew household, there were two professions which your family would probably have preferred you didn't aim for. One was prostitution (that won't surprise you) and the other was shepherding. Being a shepherd was a job for the lowest of the low. If you couldn't do anything else, you offered your services to a shepherd, to help tend the flocks. It's a fact which we're often reminded of at Christmas, because we reflect again on the kindness of a God who wanted the poorest, least-esteemed in society to be the first to hear the good news, but it's even more remarkable to reflect that Jesus called himself the 'good shepherd', that Almighty God chose to describe his relationship with the human race as that of a shepherd to his flock. To his hearers, that would have sounded like the worst kind of blasphemy.

In a world where we worry too often about status and recognition, it is worth stopping a while in wonder over this truth: the ruler of the universe loved you and me so deeply that he came to be our shepherd, to take the lowest position imaginable, simply so that we could be rescued. Having rescued us, he carries us; having carried us, he heals us; having healed us, he feeds us; having fed us, he gives us rest.

A shepherd provides everything his sheep needs. Some people ration what they ask Jesus for, not wanting to be selfish or presumptuous, but the good shepherd wants to hear it all.

LYNDALL BYWATER

FRIDAY 15 DECEMBER   **ISAIAH 60:3–22**

A colourful kingdom

'Foreigners will come to rebuild your towns, and their kings will serve you. For though I have destroyed you in my anger, I will now have mercy on you through my grace. Your gates will stay open day and night to receive the wealth of many lands.' (NLT)

When you think of heaven, what do you see? White clouds, white angels, sparkly jewels, all tastefully blended to create a sophisticatedly stylish shop-window for the Almighty? If so, then you may miss the significance of this chapter of Isaiah. You see, this is a picture of God's kingdom, of the world fully restored, and it's anything but monochrome.

The city in Isaiah 60 is a vibrant, colourful, chaotic place. There are traders, tourists and kings coming and going through its gates, day and night. It's not a predictable, closed-up place; it's a place where all are welcome, and where anything is possible. We tend to skim over all those references to Midianite camels and rams of Nebaioth because we don't really understand them, but they're crucial in this picture, because these are the cultural traditions of the lands around Israel. The Midianites were experts in rearing camels; the ships of Tarshish were legendary in their beauty and engineering; the Lebanese were highly skilled at cultivating trees. This city is a place where difference and variety are welcome, where neighbours are received with joy and where cultures work together.

If that's the kingdom we're saved to be part of, then it's a kingdom we need to be building now. When the enemy tries to scare you into thinking that different cultures mean danger or disruption, think of Isaiah 60. It's a chaotic, colourful melting-pot, but it's God's colourful, chaotic melting-pot, so it's a safe and glorious place to be.

And just as we commit ourselves to welcoming what others bring to this kingdom, so we also commit to bringing our own distinctive contributions—not blending in till we're all the same, but being ourselves and bringing our own colours to add to the stunning palette he's creating.

How monochrome is life at the moment? Do you tend to stay with the familiarity of your own culture? What could you do to expand your horizons and discover more about other cultures?

LYNDALL BYWATER

SATURDAY 16 DECEMBER   **ISAIAH 54:11–17; 65:17–25**

A happy ending

'But be glad and rejoice for ever in what I will create, for I will create Jerusalem to be a delight and its people a joy. I will rejoice over Jerusalem and take delight in my people; the sound of weeping and of crying will be heard in it no more.' (NIV)

I'm an avid reader, and I particularly love stories with a happy ending. In fact, I have read so many of them that I've started to get a feel for how they usually work. There's the beginning and middle, where things seem to go more and more wrong, and then there's the agonising crisis-point, where it looks as though everything is going to crash and burn, but then suddenly there's the beginning of the 'happy slide'—the moment when, although there's still a lot to be resolved, you just know things have turned a corner, and all that's left is to cruise joyfully towards glorious resolution.

At this time of year, Christians often get perplexed about why people seem to get so much more excited about Christmas than Easter. Is it a wilful choice to ignore the realities of Jesus' death and resurrection, or is it perhaps something to do with the fact that people sense, deep down, that Christmas is somehow the start of the 'happy slide'?

Our final prophetic picture from the Isaiah prophecies is God's creation rebuild. Whether you prefer the image of a city made of jewels, or the land where untimely death is done away with, today's readings are both versions of the same thing. The final chapter of our salvation story is a glorious putting-right of all things, in a newborn world where injustice, pain and sorrow have no place.

For centuries, God's people had heard about this land, but had seen no tangible proof that it would ever exist. The rebuilt Jerusalem certainly didn't match up. And then, one night in a dark, dusty stable, that tangible proof arrived. There would still be so much to sort out but, at last, the world was on the happy slide towards full and complete redemption.

If you find the run-up to Christmas starting to bog you down, remind yourself that you're marking the moment when salvation himself stepped into our world. In all the busyness, thank God for the happy ending that is to come.

LYNDALL BYWATER

Prophecies about Jesus

Christine Platt writes:

As we start our readings it is now the third Sunday of Advent—traditionally a time of prayer and fasting as we anticipate the celebration of Jesus' birth. Advent also signifies looking forward with even greater anticipation to Jesus' second coming when he returns, not as a baby, but in a blaze of glory as our majestic King of kings and Lord of lords—two very different 'comings'. It's another reminder that we can't put God in a box and expect him to always do things in the same way.

Scattered throughout the Old Testament are prophecies related to Jesus' birth, and throughout the whole Bible there are prophecies which speak about his second coming. It has been calculated that for every prophecy of his first coming, there are eight predicting his second coming.

For these two weeks we will look at prophecies about Jesus' birth and life. Some of these also have echoes concerning his return in power. These were written by many different authors under the inspiration of the Spirit. They appear in various books of the Old Testament and date over approximately 1000 years. One definition of prophecy is a prediction that was written years before it was fulfilled. As New Testament people we have the privilege of being able to look back to the reality which Old Testament believers could scarcely dream of. What was barely glimpsed by them has been revealed to us. 'The Word became flesh and made his dwelling among us' (John 1:14). The fact that some held on to their hope of a future Redeemer-Messiah is testimony to their tenacious faith. Many, especially in the religious hierarchy, didn't recognise Jesus when he came. Mary and Joseph, Zechariah and Elizabeth, Simeon and Anna were those whose dogged faith was rewarded by sight of this precious gift to our hopelessly broken world.

Jesus fulfilled these prophecies in minute detail. The probability of anyone fulfilling all these prophecies by sheer chance is infinitesimal. God's plan and purpose were set in motion before the creation of the world. The fulfilment of all these prophecies gives us confidence in the reliability of Scripture and in God's continuing good hand upon this world. I pray these readings will strengthen your faith and give hope for the future.

Jesus—God's Holy Son

'You are my Son; today I have become your father. Ask me and I will make the nations your inheritance, the ends of the earth your possession.' (NIV)

This Psalm is called a royal psalm and was originally composed for the coronation of Davidic kings. It is also applied to Christ as the great son of David and God's anointed.

The full identity of Jesus is a crucial issue for believers today. Jesus himself asked his disciples, '"Who do you say I am?" Simon Peter answered, "You are the Messiah, the Son of the living God"' (Matthew 16:15–16). Jesus knew that his disciples needed fully to understand who he was before they could make sense of what he was doing, and what would happen to him.

Some people today would have us believe that Jesus was just a good man, a healer and teacher who left us an example to follow. All of those attributes are true, but his sacrifice on the cross makes no sense unless he was the holy one of God. No human being could pay the price of sin, however well-intentioned they might be.

Psalm 2:12 instructs us to 'Kiss [the Lord's] son, or he will be angry and your way will lead to your destruction… Blessed are all who take refuge in him.' To 'kiss' is a sign of submission to another's lordship. We dare not diminish Jesus in any way by reducing him to a teacher and healer. He is co-equal with God the Father and God the Holy Spirit.

The apostle John states bluntly: 'In the beginning was the Word, and the Word was with God and the Word was God. He was with God in the beginning' (John 1:1–2). The Old and New Testaments bear witness to the fact that the one who was to come is none other than God himself, worthy of honour, praise, worship and total obedience.

Who do you say Jesus is? Have you 'kissed' him as a sign of submission to his sovereign rule over your life? Has he become more of your pal rather than your Lord? Talk to him about this.

CHRISTINE PLATT

MONDAY 18 DECEMBER   **GENESIS 12:1–9**

Jesus—a descendant of Abraham

The Lord had said to Abram… 'I will make you into a great nation and I will bless you … and all peoples on earth will be blessed through you.' (NIV)

In Matthew 1 we read: 'This is the genealogy of Jesus the Messiah the son of David, the son of Abraham.' When God spoke again to Abraham in Genesis 22:18 he reiterated, 'through your offspring all nations on earth will be blessed, because you have obeyed me'. Who else would bless and has already blessed all the nations but Jesus?—this very special 'offspring' of his revered ancestor, Abraham.

Genealogical lists tend to produce a yawn in some of us and we are tempted to skip those pages. However, the Jewish people take great pride in tracing back their ancestry. Many people today are fascinated by investigating their family tree. If I discovered some illustrious forebears I might also be quite chuffed! It would be inspiring to look back and know that your ancestors had done something grand—made some medical discovery, written a classic book or won an Olympic medal—or that I was related to royalty. But actually, even non-Jews can claim Abraham as their ancestor. 'If you belong to Christ, then you are Abraham's seed, and heirs according to the promise' (Galatians 3:29).

We have been grafted into the genealogy starting with Abraham, right through to Jesus, to us today! We have stirring examples of men and women of faith, courage and obedience to look back to. Maybe your physical family tree is not exceptional, but spiritually you are top-notch! You come from a magnificent dynasty of heroes just as Jesus did! Note that this astounding promise was given to Abraham because he had obeyed God. That's the example our spiritual ancestors have left us to follow so that we also can play a part in being a blessing to the nations.

Read through Hebrews 11. Recognise and be grateful that these people are your lost-long relatives. Be encouraged by their faith and be determined to walk in their footsteps.

CHRISTINE PLATT

TUESDAY 19 DECEMBER   **REVELATION 5:1–14**

Jesus—Lion of the tribe of Judah

'One of the twenty-four elders said to me, "Stop weeping! Look, the Lion of the tribe of Judah, the heir to David's throne, has won the victory."' (NLT)

In Jacob's last words of blessing to his son Judah, he proclaimed: 'The sceptre will not depart from Judah, nor the ruler's staff from his descendants, until the coming of the one to whom it belongs, the one whom all nations will honour' (Genesis 49:10).

About 1400 years later this prophecy was fulfilled in Jesus' birth (Luke 3:23–37). In Revelation 5:13 the apostle John hears in that magnificent future time 'every creature in heaven and on earth and under the earth and in the sea' sing praise and honour to Jesus.

Jacob also refers to Judah as a lion, and in Revelation we read of Jesus as the lion and the lamb. What a paradox—the king of the jungle and the defenceless sacrificial lamb!

This reminds me of the scene in C.S. Lewis' book, *The Lion, the Witch and the Wardrobe*, where Aslan, the lion, submits himself to be killed. The witch's gleeful celebration party is cut short when Aslan triumphs over death and breaks the witch's power over the land and its people.

The baby whose birth we will soon celebrate became both the lion and the lamb. He is the mighty King of kings, but also the Lamb of God who takes away the sin of the world (John 1:29). On the cross with his final breath Jesus said, 'It is finished!' (John 19:30). He meant every syllable. Satan's power is defeated. We are free. Let's not allow Satan a foothold in our lives by wilful sin or false guilt. Let's live in true freedom—it is our Christian birthright.

Lord Jesus Christ, I praise you for being willing to be the sacrificial lamb for me. By your mighty lion power I resist any attempt of the enemy to pull me away from loving you with all my heart.

CHRISTINE PLATT

WEDNESDAY 20 DECEMBER   **JEREMIAH 23:1–8**

Jesus—descendant of King David

'For the time is coming, says the Lord, when I will raise up a righteous descendant from King David's line. He will be a King who rules with wisdom… This will be his name: "The Lord Is Our Righteousness."' (NLT)

This prophecy from the mouth of Jeremiah was written sometime between 626 and 586 BC and was fulfilled by the birth of Jesus about 2000 years ago. Matthew 1:1 states: 'This is a record of the ancestors of Jesus, the Messiah, a descendant of David.' Many people were descendants of David, but none other is worthy of the name—'The Lord Is Our Righteousness', and none other is a king who always rules with wisdom.

King David is regarded as one of Israel's greatest kings, yet he would never have claimed those titles for himself. David's failures are clearly spelled out as is his heartfelt contrition (Psalm 51). He received forgiveness and God gave him this mind-blowing character reference: 'I have found David son of Jesse, a man after my own heart. He will do everything I want him to do' (Acts 13:22). Wow!

David's story gives hope to all of us who have failed. Maybe our failures are not as public as David's, but we know what they are and so does God. He is ready to forgive us just as he did David. Foolishly, David attempted to hide his misdeeds, as if that were possible, but God did not let him continue to wallow in his sin. When we fall, the only thing to do is to be honest, confess it to God and to people if that's appropriate. It's humbling, and most of us don't like being humbled, but it's the only way to freedom and restoration of authentic relationship with God and with those around us.

Jesus proved himself worthy of the title: 'The Lord Is Our Righteousness' by his supreme sacrifice on the cross. 'Christ's one act of righteousness brings a right relationship with God and new life for everyone' (Romans 5:18).

Is there something you need to repent of? Read through Psalm 51. Follow David's example and receive the forgiveness and restoration for which Jesus paid such a high price.

CHRISTINE PLATT

THURSDAY 21 DECEMBER MATTHEW 3:1–17

Jesus—anointed by the Holy Spirit

As soon as Jesus was baptised… heaven was opened, and he saw the Spirit of God descending like a dove and alighting on him. And a voice from heaven said, 'This is my Son, whom I love; with him I am well pleased.' (NIV)

Isaiah 11:2 records the prophecy about the Spirit of the Lord 'resting' on the Messiah, and at Jesus' baptism this prophecy was fulfilled. The Spirit is described as having wisdom, understanding, counsel, power, knowledge and the fear of the Lord.

The mind-boggling truth is that all those who trust in Jesus have the self-same Spirit with all those wonderful attributes! And because of Jesus God says also to us: 'This is my son or daughter, whom I love; with them I am well pleased.' We are loved by Almighty God, we have been given the Holy Spirit—truly we are privileged and blessed people. But it doesn't always feel like that, does it?

Our enemy wants to cast doubt on these facts. He insinuates in our ears: 'How could God love you? You are a failure. You have no power to live rightly and please God.' These are lies, and we need to arm ourselves with truth. The Bible tells us time and time again how much God loves us and how precious we are to him. 'I have loved you with an everlasting love. I have drawn you with unfailing kindness' (Jeremiah 31:3). And God didn't wait for us to make an effort to be good enough—he would have had to wait a very long time! 'But God demonstrates his own love for us in this: while we were still sinners, Christ died for us' (Romans 5:8). God saw the mess that humanity was in, yet he did not reject us but had compassion and sent us our Saviour-Redeemer.

God's consuming passion is to love us. Sadly we often doubt that and pull away, rather than running into his enveloping arms for reassurance, forgiveness and guidance.

Memorise a verse about God's love and embed it in your mind and heart. Take your place today as one of God's beloved ones with whom he is well pleased, and kick Satan's lies out of your life.

CHRISTINE PLATT

FRIDAY 22 DECEMBER   **LUKE 1:5–25**

John the Baptist—the forerunner

'He will go on before the Lord, in the spirit and power of Elijah, to turn the hearts of the parents to their children and the disobedient to the wisdom of the righteous—to make ready a people prepared for the Lord.' (NIV)

There was huge excitement in the Zechariah and Elizabeth household! An angel had prophesied that they would have a miracle child in their old age. And not just any child, this one was extra special. He would serve God in the spirit and power of Elijah.

Their minds would have leapt instantly to the writings of the prophet Malachi: 'I will send you the prophet Elijah before that great and dreadful day of the Lord comes. He will turn the hearts of the parents to their children, and the hearts of the children to their parents (4:5). The NIV Study Bible (p. 1400) notes that: 'As Elijah came before Elisha so Elijah will be sent to prepare God's people for the Lord's coming. John the Baptist ministered "in the spirit and power of Elijah."'

Nine months later Zechariah and Elizabeth's longed-for son was born. Despite much opposition he faithfully carried out the ministry God had assigned him: 'to make ready a people prepared for the Lord'. Jesus himself validated John as recorded in Matthew 11:11, 14 (NIV): 'Among those born of women there has not risen anyone greater than John the Baptist… And, if you are willing to accept it, he is the Elijah who was to come.'

In the same remarkable way God has assigned each of us a role in making ready a people prepared for the Lord, and we also go in the power of the Holy Spirit, just as John did. We tread in illustrious footprints! We may not experience crowds of people flocking to hear our message, but our lives will impact those around us whether they are our family, friends, workmates, neighbours, those with whom we have a chance encounter in shops or on the street. Is that impact contributing towards preparing people to trust in Jesus?

Look with fresh eyes on all whom you meet today. Are your life, your words, actions and attitudes attracting people to Jesus? Do people ask you questions about your values and beliefs? Talk with him about this.

CHRISTINE PLATT

SATURDAY 23 DECEMBER   **LUKE 1:26–45**

Jesus—born of a virgin

'How will this be,' Mary asked the angel, 'since I am a virgin?' The angel answered, 'The Holy Spirit will come on you, and the power of the Most High will overshadow you. So the holy one to be born will be called the Son of God.' (NIV)

Devout Jews had long pondered the message brought by Isaiah sometime between 701 and 681BC: 'The Lord himself will give you a sign: The virgin will conceive and give birth to a son, and will call him Immanuel' (Isaiah 7:14). Immanuel means 'God with us'. Few dreamed that God would choose a young peasant girl from an insignificant poor village in whom to birth his holy one.

In Mary God found a teenager with outrageous faith. After asking one fairly basic question, she believed that what God said would actually happen. Somehow, even though she was not yet married she would become the mother of this long-awaited God-Man. She believed the Angel Gabriel's extraordinary words: 'For no word from God will ever fail.' She must have frequently needed to remind herself of that declaration over the intervening months. As her pregnancy started to show, surely she had some anxious moments about how her family would react as well as her friends and neighbours? She had the joy and relief of seeing God deal with these natural concerns, especially in relation to Joseph.

Maybe you are facing a faith challenge and you wonder how it is going to turn out. Is there light at the end of the tunnel? Gabriel's words are still relevant for your problem today. When we worry and fret and have sleepless nights we are basically saying: 'This issue is too big for God to deal with; this person is too difficult; this financial crisis is too huge'.

Mary had little idea of what was ahead of her, but she went forward in faith and did experience that nothing was too hard for God, and that God's grace was sufficient—because his power is made perfect in weakness (2 Corinthians 12:9).

Almighty God, with your help I choose to believe that nothing is too hard for you. You know the challenge I'm facing. The problems seem insurmountable but I choose to trust in your power and experience your all-sufficient grace.

CHRISTINE PLATT

SUNDAY 24 DECEMBER   **LUKE 2:1–7**

Jesus—born in Bethlehem

So Joseph also went up from the town of Nazareth in Galilee to Judea, to Bethlehem the town of David, because he belonged to the house and line of David. He went there to register with Mary, who was pledged to be married to him and was expecting a child. (NIV)

Bethlehem, though a small village south of the vastly more impressive city of Jerusalem where the rulers had their palaces, was chosen by God to be the birthplace of this unique baby who would change the world and become known as King of kings and Lord of lords. 'But you, Bethlehem Ephrathah, though you are small among the clans of Judah, out of you will come for me one who will be ruler over Israel, whose origins are from of old, from ancient times' (Micah 5:2).

Bethlehem had other claims to fame. Ruth and Naomi settled there after coming from Moab. Ruth and Boaz's son, Obed, was born there and became part of the lineage of King David. Samuel the prophet was sent to Bethlehem to anoint David king over Israel. It had royal connections, even though in the world's eyes it was insignificant.

However, Mary and Joseph lived in Nazareth. How was God going to get heavily pregnant Mary and her fiancé Joseph to Bethlehem? As we know nothing is impossible with God, so Caesar Augustus was prompted to call for a census, so 'everyone went to their own town to register'. I'm grateful that our present-day census is carried out with less hassle for us all! Mary and Joseph had no choice but to make this difficult and potentially dangerous journey to bring Jesus into the world. They might have been tempted to wonder why God's provision of the birth place was so inconvenient.

For most of us in the developed world the thought of giving birth alone in an unhygienic cave or stable is unthinkable. We would be phoning emergency services. Yet in the developing world this is not unusual.

As we remember Jesus being born, let's pray for mothers who have to walk miles to a clinic or give birth alone with no access to medical help. Ask God to watch over them just as he did for Mary.

CHRISTINE PLATT

MONDAY 25 DECEMBER   **JOHN 1:1–18**

Jesus—God with us

The Word was with God, and the Word was God… So the Word became human and made his home among us. He was full of unfailing love and faithfulness. And we have seen his glory, the glory of the Father's one and only Son. (NLT)

We have already seen the prophecy in Isaiah 7:14 that the child would be called Immanuel, which means God with us. These verses in John's Gospel underline that truth. The babe whose birth we celebrate today was truly the omniscient God who limited himself to a physical human body. 'The Word became human and made his home among us.' For 30 years he lived in relative obscurity—being a good son, an elder brother to his siblings and making and repairing furniture and farming implements. As a devout Jewish boy he studied the Hebrew Scriptures.

I wonder if Mary grew impatient as to when he would reveal himself to his people Israel. They certainly needed a Saviour/Redeemer/King. But Jesus waited until the time was right. We have the immense advantage of being able to look back over history and trace God's impeccably timed actions. Even though we may sometimes chafe at delays, his timing is spot on. We're often the ones who are out of step. On a really basic level, taking a cake out of the oven before it's cooked ruins the whole thing. How much more, in big decisions, we need to be led by Immanuel—God with us. He knows the right time to achieve the best outcome.

Seven hundred years before Jesus came his birth was predicted in minute detail. Today as we celebrate the Word becoming human and making his home among us, let's aim to respect God's timetable in all areas of our lives. Let's remember that God will not be rushed, however much we fret and moan. He has proved time and time again that he is working to a celestial timetable and, if we're wise, we will submit to that and not attempt to force our own agenda.

Mighty Jesus, Immanuel, forgive my impatience and for so often telling you what to do. With your help I will submit to your plans, your purposes and your timetable this day and every day.

CHRISTINE PLATT

TUESDAY 26 DECEMBER **MATTHEW 2:1–15**

Jesus—refugee in Egypt

After the wise men were gone, an angel of the Lord appeared to Joseph in a dream. 'Get up! Flee to Egypt with the child and his mother ... Stay there until I tell you to return, because Herod is going to search for the child to kill him.' (NLT)

Joseph had already had one encounter with an angel and knew prompt obedience was called for. He probably also knew the prophecy in Hosea 11:1: 'Out of Egypt I called my son.' This prophecy initially applied to the whole nation of Israel which was rescued from Egypt and led back to the promised land by Moses. Matthew sees the correlation between Israel as a nation and the child who was to become Israel's king.

Immediately Joseph escaped to Egypt with Mary and Jesus. This was no small undertaking in those days. Today, after a few hours in a plane, your feet would touch Egyptian soil. In Jesus' day it was a long, exhausting, probably dangerous and expensive journey. I wonder if they used the gift of gold from the wise men to finance the trip. Nothing is known about the life this family lived in Egypt. No doubt they searched for a community of Jewish people with whom to live and Joseph set up shop as a carpenter. And there they waited for the next angelic message.

Jesus faced a formidable foe in the megalomaniacal Herod, but Jesus' divine protector was even more formidable. We also face enemies in our lives—some human, but all originating from the enemy of our souls. Do you sometimes get angry and fight against those who oppose you and forget that the real aggressor is Satan? Ephesians 6:12 states: 'For we are not fighting against fresh-and-blood enemies, but against evil rulers and authorities of the unseen world, against mighty powers in this dark world, and against evil spirits in the heavenly places.'

In this time of joyous celebration, let's remember that Satan doesn't take holidays. In Christ we have victory, but we need to be alert to recognise Satan's attacks.

Read slowly and thoughtfully through Ephesians 6:10–18. When you feel angry and want to react with hostility, remind yourself who the real enemy is. Recognise Satan's activity and take your fight to the Lord.

CHRISTINE PLATT

WEDNESDAY 27 DECEMBER MATTHEW 2:16–23

Jesus—born among sorrow

When Herod realised that he had been outwitted by the Magi, he was furious, and he gave orders to kill all the boys in Bethlehem and its vicinity who were two years old and under, in accordance with the time he had learned from the Magi. (NIV)

Thwarted by the wise men, Herod lashed out. All the boys under two in Bethlehem and the surrounding areas were slaughtered on the altar of his pride and fear of being usurped. What a sick individual he was. But, as we know, the driving force that propelled him to such extreme brutality was Satan. The birth that was to bring joy and hope to all the world was accompanied by wrenching heartache, sorrow and tears. Those grieving mothers and fathers would have had no understanding of the cosmic struggle surrounding them and their babies.

On occasion God lets us in on the reason why bad things happen to us, but most times he does not. We are left with incomprehension and that makes closure and acceptance even harder.

All we can be sure of is that God does know and one day, either here or in eternity, all questions will be answered and we will understand the reasons behind it all. It's like a piece of embroidery. From the back it looks messy, but when you look at the front the full intricate picture is revealed. The dark colours accentuate and bring definition to the subtler shades. Every colour and stitch is necessary to create the perfect finished article.

I find that a helpful counterbalance to the plaintive 'Why?' that escapes my lips. Somehow it is all going to work out. I just need to hang in there, trust God and allow him to bring the colours and textures into my life that he decides will best benefit his kingdom work. Certainly easier said than done. But God promises that his grace is sufficient for us today just as it was for those parents in Bethlehem.

God, the Master Designer—I surrender to what you allow in my life even when I don't understand why things happen. I know you don't design evil, but you can transform it into something beautiful and noble.

CHRISTINE PLATT

THURSDAY 28 DECEMBER   **LUKE 19:28–44**

Jesus—the king comes

They brought it to Jesus, threw their cloaks on the colt and put Jesus on it. As he went along, people spread their cloaks on the road… 'Blessed is the king who comes in the name of the Lord!' (NIV)

Jesus deliberately enacts the prophecy in Zechariah 9:9: 'Rejoice greatly, Daughter Zion!… See, your king comes to you, righteous and victorious, lowly and riding on a donkey, on a colt, the foal of a donkey.'

In this deeply symbolic act Jesus gave even more evidence that he was the Messiah. Yet he knew that these same people who were so thrilled to see him would soon be yelling 'Crucify him!' No wonder he wept, 'If you, even you, had only known on this day what would bring you peace—but now it is hidden from your eyes… You did not recognise the time of God's coming to you' (vv. 41, 44).

The significance of this event was lost on most of the cheering crowd. They were keen to experience his miracles and listen to his teaching, but had not yet bowed the knee in submission to him as Lord of their lives.

Many of us can be like that. We want the blessings; we want to go to heaven when we die; we want our prayers answered. But sadly we can resemble the seed planted on rocky ground (Matthew 13:20–21). As soon as difficulties come and life does not pan out the way we hope, our faith falters. And yet it is in those faith-stretching times that God draws close to us, to guide, to empower, to comfort and if we turn to him our relationship with him will grow stronger and become more precious. Still many of us turn away. We don't recognise the time of God's coming to us. We don't see trials as an opportunity to experience more of God. We see them as something to avoid.

When you encounter problems, try asking God: 'What are you inviting me to think or feel or do through this situation? How can I see this from your point of view?' This will give you a different perspective.

CHRISTINE PLATT

FRIDAY 29 DECEMBER   **JOHN 13:18–30**

Jesus—betrayed by a friend

'I am not referring to all of you; I know those I have chosen. But this is to fulfil the passage of Scripture: "He who shares my bread has turned against me."'… As soon as Judas took the bread, Satan entered into him. (NIV)

Have you ever been betrayed, unjustly accused or rejected by a friend or loved one? It really hurts, doesn't it? You remember the happy moments of friendship and shared fun, and then somehow it all turns sour. For some deranged reason Judas decided to betray his friend and of course Jesus knew all about it. The detailed prophecies about being betrayed by a friend for 30 pieces of silver and the purchase of the potter's field are contained in Psalm 41:9 and Zechariah 11:12–13.

What always astounds me is the depth of Jesus' understanding and compassion in his dealings with Judas. Even knowing he would turn against him, Jesus allowed him to continue to look after the money. He washed Judas' feet and then included him in that holy moment of the Last Supper. Jesus reached out and pursued him in every way possible but, alas, to no avail. Eventually Jesus had to leave Judas to bear the consequences of his actions. Jesus' love was pure and his wisdom was infinite yet he couldn't convince Judas to change his mind about him.

Rejection can also happen to us sometimes. With our limited human resources, we try with God's help to mend and build relationships even when it hurts, yet the other person will not bend. In order to preserve our own emotional and spiritual health, there may come a time when we have to leave our erstwhile friend to their own devices. Our enemy wants us to feel guilty for 'giving up' on our friend. The antidote to that is to continue to pray for them, asking God to intervene with his infinite love, wisdom and power. When we've done all we can, we can safely and freely leave them in God's hands (see Romans 12:17–18).

Heavenly Father, I bring my friend to you. You know all that's happened. Please guard me from false guilt and help me to pray faithfully for them. They are your child and your responsibility, not mine.

CHRISTINE PLATT

SATURDAY 30 DECEMBER **2 CORINTHIANS 5:11–21**

Jesus—enabled reconciliation with God

We are therefore Christ's ambassadors, as though God were making his appeal through us. We implore you on Christ's behalf: be reconciled to God. God made him who had no sin to be sin for us, so that in him we might become the righteousness of God. (NIV)

Christ's death was not some dreadful mistake. It was a necessity prophesied from eternity past. 'But he was pierced for our transgressions, he was crushed for our iniquities; the punishment that brought us peace was upon him, and by his wounds we are healed' (Isaiah 53:5). God knew we needed a Saviour and he provided one in Jesus.

Jesus was born with a monumental weight of expectation on him. In his humanity he had to resist every attack of Satan so that he could fulfil his destiny as the holy sacrifice for all the sins of every human being who has ever lived—sins past, present and future. I get a bit overwhelmed with my own numerous sins, let alone those of billions of people. Jesus made possible our reconciliation with our heavenly Father. Now, he asks us to carry on his work: 'he has committed to us the message of reconciliation' (v. 19).

For many people Christmas and New Year may be the only times their thoughts turn to spiritual matters. Are we making the most of this once-a-year opportunity? In the aftermath of Christmas and as our minds turn to the new year ahead, ask God to enable you to be an ambassador for him in 2018. As ambassadors represent their country, so we represent Christ. Is your life increasingly perfumed with the fragrance of Jesus so that others are drawn to him? Talk with Jesus about this.

The past is gone, the future beckons. Don't allow the past to limit your future. God's purpose is for you to be an agent of reconciliation and, if you are willing, he will make it happen. He has already accomplished the really difficult part and he invites our participation.

Lord Jesus, thank you for being a willing sacrifice so I could become friends with your Father. Enable me to be an agent of reconciliation for you in 2018. Let me have the privilege of ushering someone into your kingdom.

CHRISTINE PLATT

SUNDAY 31 DECEMBER   LUKE 24:1–12, 36–53

Jesus—he has risen!

[Jesus] said to them, 'This is what I told you while I was still with you: everything must be fulfilled that is written about me in the Law of Moses, the Prophets and the Psalms.' Then he opened their minds so they could understand the Scriptures. (NIV)

The disciples, the women and others were emotionally wrung out, grief-stricken, feeling guilty for having run away, confused and lost. All at once Jesus was standing there with them! He gave them the reassurance of his presence. He pointed them to the evidence that he was real and alive—his hands, his feet and, with glorious normality, he ate some fish! Then he opened their minds to understand the Scriptures—some of the prophecies are in Psalm 16:9–11 and Isaiah 53:10–11.

They'd spent three years with him and seen him do all sorts of miracles—healings, deliverances, overturning the rules of nature—stilling the storm, multiplying food—yet for him to be alive again after his horrific death was so hard for them to accept.

Yet, as he opened their minds to understand, suddenly it all made sense! The prophecies fitted into place. He truly was their Lord and friend, risen from the dead. They wouldn't have grasped all the details but they did realise that Jesus had accomplished his purpose on earth—to make possible the forgiveness of sins. He was now leaving them as witnesses to all the nations. That new understanding and renewed appreciation of who Jesus was energised them to accept this colossal role with joy and reverence, even though he was taken away from them up to heaven.

When I feel overwhelmed, fearful or confused it usually means I've lost sight of the immensity of Jesus' love and his willingness to come alongside with support and help. Jesus does not intend for us to struggle alone. He is the God of the breakthrough. The song 'Turn your eyes upon Jesus' comes to mind. What better motto with which to start the New Year!

Use this chorus to encourage your heart today: 'Turn your eyes upon Jesus, Look full in his wonderful face. And the things of earth will grow strangely dim in the light of his glory and grace' (Helen Lemmel, 1863–1961).

CHRISTINE PLATT

Recommended reading

The songs Luke records in his inspired Gospel—the songs of Mary, Zechariah, Simeon, and the angels at Bethlehem—reveal the wonderful truth that 'in the town of David a Saviour has been born to us'. Acclaimed writer and speaker Derek Tidball leads us through these songs demonstrating the gracious purposes of God that they celebrate in the birth of Jesus Christ.

Christmas through the Keyhole
Luke's glimpses of Advent
Derek Tidball
978 0 85746 520 7 £6.99
brfonline.org.uk

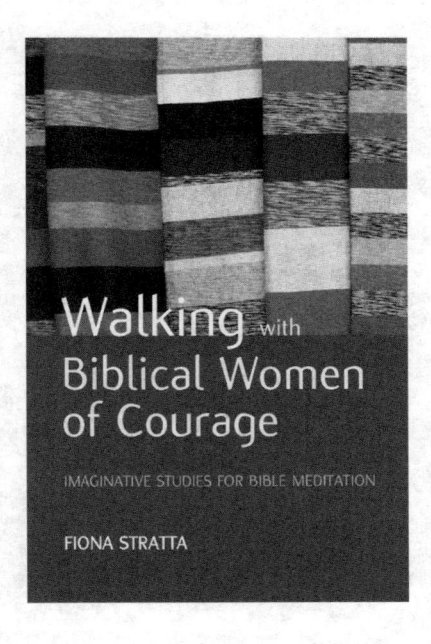

We're all called to everyday courage: perseverance in suffering, resilience in the face of disappointment and loss, strength to take on difficult roles. *Walking with Biblical Women of Courage* is an encouraging and empowering collection of meditative monologues told from the perspectives of women from both the Old and New Testaments.

Walking with Biblical Women of Courage
Imaginative studies for Bible meditation
Fiona Stratta
978 0 85746 533 7 £7.99
brfonline.org.uk

Wanda Nash, a well-established writer on spirituality in her late 70s, extends a compelling invitation to grow old boldly. The book includes Wanda's reflection on her encounter later in life with terminal cancer. Demonstrating a profound sense of the value and purposefulness of 'old age', her indomitable spirit is matched only by her fresh vision of the love of God in Jesus Christ.

Come, Let Us Age!
An invitation to grow old boldly
Wanda Nash
978 0 85746 558 0 £6.99
brfonline.org.uk

To order

Online: **brfonline.org.uk**
Tel.: +44 (0)1865 319700
Mon–Fri 9.15–17.30

Delivery times within the UK are normally 15 working days. Prices are correct at the time of going to press but may change without prior notice.

BRF

Title	Price	Qty	Total
Christmas through the Keyhole	£6.99		
Walking with Biblical Women of Courage	£7.99		
Come, Let Us Age!	£6.99		

POSTAGE AND PACKING CHARGES			
Order value	UK	Europe	Rest of world
Under £7.00	£1.25	£3.00	£5.50
£7.00–£29.99	£2.25	£5.50	£10.00
£30.00 and over	FREE	Prices on request	

Total value of books	
Postage and packing	
Total for this order	

Please complete in BLOCK CAPITALS

Title .... First name/initials .... Surname ....

Address ....

.... Postcode ....

Acc. No. .... Telephone ....

Email ....

Please keep me informed about BRF's books and resources ❑ by email ❑ by post
Please keep me informed about the wider work of BRF ❑ by email ❑ by post

Method of payment

❑ Cheque (made payable to BRF) ❑ MasterCard / Visa

Card no. ☐☐☐☐ ☐☐☐☐ ☐☐☐☐ ☐☐☐☐

Valid from [M M] [Y Y] Expires [M M] [Y Y] Security code* ☐☐☐
Last 3 digits on the reverse of the card

Signature* .... Date .... / .... / ....

*ESSENTIAL IN ORDER TO PROCESS YOUR ORDER

Please return this form with the appropriate payment to:
BRF, 15 The Chambers, Vineyard, Abingdon OX14 3FE | enquiries@brf.org.uk

To read our terms and find out about cancelling your order, please visit **brfonline.org.uk/terms**.

The Bible Reading Fellowship (BRF) is a Registered Charity (233280)

SUBSCRIPTION INFORMATION

Each issue of *Day by Day with God* is available from Christian bookshops everywhere. Copies may also be available through your church book agent or from the person who distributes Bible reading notes in your church.

Alternatively you may obtain *Day by Day with God* on subscription direct from the publishers. There are two kinds of subscription:

Individual subscriptions
covering 3 issues for 4 copies or less, payable in advance
(including postage & packing).

To order, please complete the details on page 144 and return with the appropriate payment to: BRF, 15 The Chambers, Vineyard, Abingdon OX14 3FE

You can also use the form on page 144 to order a gift subscription for a friend.

Group subscriptions
covering 3 issues for 5 copies or more, sent to **one** UK address (post free).

Please note that the annual billing period for group subscriptions runs from 1 May to 30 April.

To order, please complete the details on page 143 and return with the appropriate payment to: BRF, 15 The Chambers, Vineyard, Abingdon OX14 3FE

You will receive an invoice with the first issue of notes.

All our Bible reading notes can be ordered online by visiting
biblereadingnotes.org.uk/subscriptions

For information about our other Bible reading notes,
and apps for iPhone and iPod touch, visit
biblereadingnotes.org.uk

All subscription enquiries should be directed to:
BRF, 15 The Chambers, Vineyard, Abingdon OX14 3FE
+44 (0)1865 319700 | enquiries@brf.org.uk

DAY BY DAY WITH GOD GROUP SUBSCRIPTION FORM

> All our Bible reading notes can be ordered online by visiting
> **biblereadingnotes.org.uk/subscriptions**

The group subscription rate for *Day by Day with God* will be £13.20 per person until April 2018.

☐ I would like to take out a group subscription for .... (quantity) copies.

☐ Please start my order with the January 2018 / May 2018 / September 2018* issue. I would like to pay annually/receive an invoice* with each edition of the notes. (*delete as appropriate)

Please do not send any money with your order. Send your order to BRF and we will send you an invoice. The group subscription year is from 1 May to 30 April. If you start subscribing in the middle of a subscription year we will invoice you for the remaining number of issues left in that year.

Name and address of the person organising the group subscription:

Title .... First name/initials .... Surname ....

Address ....

.... Postcode ....

Telephone .... Email ....

Church ....

Name of Minister ....

Name and address of the person paying the invoice if the invoice needs to be sent directly to them:

Title .... First name/initials .... Surname ....

Address ....

.... Postcode ....

Telephone .... Email ....

Please return this form with the appropriate payment to:
BRF, 15 The Chambers, Vineyard, Abingdon OX14 3FE

To read our terms and find out about cancelling your order, please visit **brfonline.org.uk/terms**.

The Bible Reading Fellowship is a Registered Charity (233280)

DAY BY DAY WITH GOD INDIVIDUAL/GIFT SUBSCRIPTION FORM

To order online, please visit **biblereadingnotes.org.uk/subscriptions**

- [ ] I would like to give a gift subscription (please provide both names and addresses)
- [ ] I would like to take out a subscription myself (complete your name and address details only once)

Title .... First name/initials .... Surname ....

Address ....

.... Postcode ....

Telephone .... Email ....

Gift subscription name ....

Gift subscription address ....

.... Postcode ....

Gift message (20 words max. or include your own gift card):

....

....

Please send *Day by Day with God* beginning with the January 2018 / May 2018 / September 2018 issue (*delete as appropriate*):

(please tick box)	UK	Europe	Rest of world
Day by Day with God	☐ £16.50	☐ £24.60	☐ £28.50
2-year subscription	☐ £30.00	N/A	N/A

Total enclosed £ .... (cheques should be made payable to 'BRF')

Please charge my MasterCard / Visa ☐ Debit card ☐ with £ ....

Card no. ☐☐☐☐ ☐☐☐☐ ☐☐☐☐ ☐☐☐☐

Valid from M M Y Y   Expires M M Y Y   Security code* ☐☐☐

Last 3 digits on the reverse of the card

Signature* .... Date .... / .... / ....

*ESSENTIAL IN ORDER TO PROCESS YOUR ORDER

Please return this form with the appropriate payment to:
BRF, 15 The Chambers, Vineyard, Abingdon OX14 3FE

To read our terms and find out about cancelling your order, please visit **brfonline.org.uk/terms**.

The Bible Reading Fellowship is a Registered Charity (233280)